JL
197
.P67
M84
1983

T3-BGM-006

Where I Stand

RETIRÉ
WITHDRAWN

THIS BOOK
was donated to the CMBC Library

by *Can. Book Exchange Centre*

CANADIAN MENNONITE UNIVERSITY
LIBRARY
500 SHAFTESBURY BLVD.
WINNIPEG, MANITOBA
CANADA   R3P 2N2

CANADIAN MENNONITE BIBLE COLLEGE
LIBRARY
600 SHAFTESBURY BLVD.
WINNIPEG, MANITOBA R3P 0M4

UW Library BOOK SALE

FC
631
.M84A3
M8
1983

Where I Stand

Brian Mulroney

WITHDRAWN

CANADIAN MENNONITE UNIVERSITY
LIBRARY
500 SHAFTESBURY BLVD.
WINNIPEG, MANITOBA
CANADA   R3P 2N2

LIBRARY
MINISTRY OF THE SOLICITOR
GENERAL

SEP 24 1984

BIBLIOTHÈQUE
MINISTÈRE DU SOLLICITEUR GÉNÉRAL

McClelland and Stewart

CANADIAN MENNONITE BIBLE COLLEGE
LIBRARY
600 SHAFTESBURY BLVD.
WINNIPEG, MANITOBA R3P 0M4

Copyright © 1983 McClelland and Stewart Limited

Second printing 1983

All rights reserved. The use of any part of this publication
reproduced, transmitted in any form or by any means, electronic,
mechanical, photocopying, recording, or otherwise, or stored in a
retrieval system, without the prior consent of the publisher is an
infringement of the copyright law.

McClelland and Stewart Limited
The Canadian Publishers
25 Hollinger Road
Toronto, Ontario
M4B 3G2

Royalty income from the English and French editions
of this book will be donated to charity.

Canadian Cataloguing in Publication Data
Mulroney, Brian, 1939-
    Where I stand

ISBN 0-7710-6671-6

1. Mulroney, Brian, 1939- 2. Politicians, Canada.
3. Progressive Conservative Party of Canada. I. Title.

JL197.P7M84   320.971   C83-098333-3

Printed and bound in Canada

JL
197
.P67
M84
1983
41194

Contents

Preface / 7

I   Productivity–Our Weakest Link / 9

II   Civilizing Labour Relations / 21

III   An Industrial Strategy / 32

IV   Research and Development / 38

V   Control of Government Spending / 43

VI   Reforming the Budgetary Process / 49

VII   Thoughts on the Constitution / 55

VIII The Essence of Federalism / 67

IX   Leadership Today / 72

X   A View from Baie Comeau / 80

XI   Service to Others / 85

XII   The Conservative Challenge / 90

XIII Change and Challenge / 96

Acknowledgements / 102

I dedicate this book to those men and women who are working for the kind of Canada I wish for my children, Caroline, Benedict, and Mark.

Preface

Those who read this book will be under no illusion as to where I stand. From June 1977 to March 1983, I served as president of the Iron Ore Company of Canada, a major industrial employer in Canada. Before that, I practised as a lawyer, specializing in labour-management relations. I won't talk at length about my personal background. Suffice it to say I am the third of six children of an electrician and his wife from Baie Comeau, on Quebec's North Shore, and my wife Mila and I have three children and live in Montreal.

For twenty-eight years I have been a member in good standing of the Progressive Conservative Party of Canada. Indeed, I have offered myself as the leader of that party. I am a Conservative but one does not need to wear a label to believe that governments should balance budgets; that industry, being the motor of a country, must be kept turning; that initiative should be rewarded; that relations between labour and management should be civil; that research and development are the keys to our national well-being; that the essence of federalism, or of any system of administration, is co-operation and consensus. Neither does one need to belong to a political party to believe that men and women will stand on their own two feet when given half a chance; that government must show concern – even tenderness – in dealing with the less fortunate among us; that only free men and women are able to sever the knots tied by government bureaucrats. Some of these concerns are spelled out in the pages that follow.

This volume began with a letter from Jack McClelland of the publishers McClelland and Stewart. Jack had read an article I wrote for *Chimo* magazine and suggested that I expand my views on productivity and industrial strategy into a book. Pressures of

7

work and family prevented me from writing a manuscript afresh within his time schedule. Instead, I offered him a collection of several addresses I have given, some in English and some in French, over the last number of years. It does not purport to answer every specific issue of today.

In these addresses I have tried to speak to such fundamental concerns as unemployment, declining productivity, and inefficient government bureaucracy. These will continue to plague Canadians in the future unless we demonstrate the courage to deal with them head on.

The Iron Ore Company of Canada is a major supplier to the steel industry, and indirectly to the automobile industry. During my years there, I became intimately aware of problems facing Canada's resource and manufacturing industries, in particular problems of productivity and transportation. I was constantly reminded of the unique relationship Canada has with the United States. This special relationship is complex, stimulating, and challenging, with vital implications for our trade, economic development, environment, mutual defence, and technological advance. I have spent countless hours analysing and discussing these implications with leaders from American business, labour, finance, and state and national governments. I have been privileged, as well, to put forward the Canadian view on these and other subjects to influential groups throughout the United States.

My travels, first as a lawyer and then as a businessman, have brought me into personal contact with government leaders in countries such as China and England, Japan and Romania, France and Brazil, with their diverse interests and trade patterns. These meetings, involving discussions of the Canadian role and presence throughout the world, have been of great value to me in formulating opinions and policy analysis in international affairs.

Canada is a splendid country, and I believe we can overcome the difficulties we face on many fronts with new vision, new direction, and new hope for Canadians. It lies ahead of us to ensure that we provide both the leadership and the programs to accomplish this.

Chapter I
Productivity – Our Weakest Link

On March 27, 1982, the *Globe and Mail* carried the following story on page one: "Prime Minister Trudeau confessed yesterday that Canada is moving inexorably to a high cost economy that will not be internationally competitive when the world starts to pull out of recession.

"When we come out of this period of our economic cycle," said the Prime Minister, "we will find ourselves crowded out on the world markets by products from countries that have been able to control their costs."

Well, the Prime Minister was wrong when he said years ago that he had "wrestled inflation to the ground." He was wrong again when he announced later that "separatism is dead." He was wrong when he bad-mouthed Robert Stanfield on wage-and-price controls, only to implement them after the election of 1974. He was wrong to engineer the defeat of a Clark government over an eighteen-cent-a-gallon increase only to implement a seventy-five-cent one himself. He was wrong on these and a host of other matters. But with his statement on March 27, he was right on – proving, I suppose, that the law of averages catches up with everyone.

Canada is indeed moving inexorably to a high-cost economy which will price us out of international markets. But this situation did not happen overnight. If I were not a gentleman, I might ask: "Who's been minding the store around here these last fifteen years?" In Mr. Trudeau's fifteen years as Prime Minister, he has been thoroughly consistent in one important area – he has consistently produced deficits. Our national economic wizard has managed the remarkable feat of transforming a $500-million deficit in 1968 into about a $26-billion overrun this year.

Persistent governmental deficits on a rising scale in good times and bad led to rising prices accelerating with the passage of time. Monetary policy during this same period accommodated the rising prices by increasing the money supply above and beyond what was required to finance real growth and output. For many years savers and investors were penalized and borrowers and speculators were rewarded. In time this led to deeply imbedded inflationary expectations that contributed further to rising prices and an ever-increasing spiral of costs.

One of the most serious consequences for our economy as a whole was poor productivity performance. How does this come about? A worker finds himself falling behind as rising prices erode the real value of his earnings. Instead of working harder, he fights to increase his money wage. This raises costs and makes investment less rewarding. It also leads to industrial unrest which, too, makes investment less profitable and more risky. The saver finds that the return on his savings declines in real terms and that his capital when he is repaid has eroded in value. This discourages him from saving and thus reduces the flow of funds available for investment. He sees his friends and neighbours benefiting from the inflationary gain in the value of real property or commodities they have purchased, and he in turn is led to engage in non-productive speculative activity rather than the slow, difficult, but solid process of saving to enhance his position.

The industrialist or entrepreneur who, together with his workers, provides the true source of productivity and economic growth, such as his pool of depreciation allowances, is insufficient to finance new and up-to-date capital equipment. He is taxed on paper profits that are not real profits when adjusted for inflation. He is forced to postpone new investments and try to make do with his antiquated plant and equipment. This inevitably leads to poor productivity performance. He is unable to remain competitive and this leads to declining employment opportunities. He, too, is tempted to look for easier ways of solving his problems than the long, difficult process of building, innovating, and investing in modern plant and equipment. He looks for opportunities to take over other existing businesses at prices that are considerably below

10

replacement costs because of low real profitability that characterizes an inflationary environment.

Simply put, inflation leads to a misallocation of resources away from productive activity and toward speculative activity.

• The first thing, then, that we have to do to get our national house in order is to deal with inflation. This requires a disciplined fiscal policy, i.e., less government spending, fewer giveaway programs, and a taxation system that rewards effort and provides adequate incentives for hard work and investment. It also requires that we maintain a disciplined monetary policy, i.e., gradual reduction in the rate of increase in the money supply until a point is reached where only enough money is created to finance real increases in production.

For some years, I have been trying in public statements – with a remarkably modest degree of success – to draw attention to what I perceive to be the single most fundamental weakness of our economy. This weakness is our anemic productivity.

People constantly discuss such problems as unemployment, interest rates, and plant closings. These are very serious matters, but they are in my judgement the symptoms, not the causes, of a sick economy. The principal cause of the sickness is a gravely deteriorating productivity factor which has already crippled vast sectors of the Canadian economy. It requires our urgent and collective attention. Our failure to come to grips with this all-pervasive and socially complex problem will place us, I fear, irreversibly on a treadmill to economic oblivion.

The definition of productivity is pretty uncomplicated. Productivity is what you get out for what you put in, in capital, resources, and labour. Productivity is not a judgement on how hard people are working. It is a measurement of efficiency – how intelligently and innovatively industry uses each of the elements that go into creating a product or service. That measurement – GNP or gross national product per worker – determines total income. In the words of Rowland Frazee of the Royal Bank, who knows about productivity, "It is what a nation lives on, and it is all it lives on."

During the quarter century following World War II, Canadians enjoyed productivity increases averaging almost 2.5 per cent annually. We then dropped to 0.2 per cent per year during the late

1970s. For the last three years, to use a bookkeeping term, we have been "in the red." Unless this sickness is isolated, its growth arrested, and the problem ultimately cured, the symptoms will always remain. They may vary in size and severity depending upon the latest wonder drug or artificial prop, but they will not disappear. The symptoms may even become so socially debilitating as to cause them to be viewed as the illness itself, thus obscuring reality and inhibiting effective remedial action. Such is the situation in Canada today, with historically high unemployment, inflation, and interest rates.

There will be no solid economic recovery on which a soundly conceived national industrial strategy can be based until such time as we accept the proposition that the production of quality goods and services at internationally competitive prices is Canada's unquestioned principal challenge. Management, labour, and government must unite to meet this overriding national concern. The acknowledgement that this is the problem to be tackled is the beginning of wisdom.

The designing of innovative strategies to overcome the serious structural problems and attitudinal obstacles in government, management, and unions will test the ingenuity and resolve of all concerned. But in my view the reasonable and equitable resolution of the productivity crisis in Canada will bring about an enduring industrial recovery, just as surely as summer follows spring.

One of the great burdens this country has had to bear has been the extravagant optimism of some of our leaders. Sir Wilfrid Laurier, for example, proclaimed that "the twentieth century belongs to Canada." Our problem is that we believed him, literally. We could peddle our resources to the highest bidder, adopt any social policy of popular currency, display a degree of profligacy in public spending that would cause even the most irresponsible to blush, make erratic changes in basic taxation structure, torpedo the entire oil and gas industry, hobble the Canadian entrepreneurial spirit, and make unwelcome the foreign investor, and it did not matter – because we knew, way down deep, that the twentieth century belonged to us. With fewer than seventeen years to go, it appears likely historians will conclude that even Sir Wilfrid was occasionally given to wishful thinking. As we view the world from our diminished and diminishing position on the international economic scale, we now know that it has not happened.

So what does all this mean? It does not necessarily mean that we have to work harder, although I am not in any way offended by that prospect. It does mean that we have to work smarter. Very simply put, it comes down to this: Canadians must be encouraged to research and develop the most useful widget in the world. It must be of high quality. It must be cheaper than widgets produced elsewhere. To the extent possible, it should be an attractive, salable commodity. There must be a reliable and uninterrupted supply of such products, thereby eliminating escalating inventory costs and inducing customer satisfaction. The workers must be handsomely rewarded for their efforts in making this possible. They must receive good wages and benefits, a share of the profits, and tax incentives to invest in their own company and share in its success, thereby solidifying the indispensable process of commonality of purpose and eliminating the adversarial system of labour relations.

The capital investors, corporate or otherwise, must be made to feel welcome by government. Their risk must be generously rewarded. Their job-creation skills and capacities must be viewed as vital to the nation. Their consequent obligation toward enhanced job security for their employees becomes a logical and desirable end result.

Governments at all levels must learn that they have no money – it is our money. They must, therefore, exercise frugality and prudence in its use, leaving as much as possible in the hands of the only wealth-producers and job-creators in Canada – namely the widget-makers.

The taxing power of government should be used sparingly and innovatively as an instrument of industrial expansion and national development to encourage, to nurture, and to reward the productive, the creative, and the daring elements in our society. The tragic process of the swedenizing of Canada must come to a halt. If I wanted to live in Sweden, I would move there. I am a Canadian and want to be free, to the extent reasonably possible, of government intrusion and direction and regimentation and bureaucratic overkill. I do not want to be one of twenty-four million homogenized Canadians. I want to be unfettered and concerned and imaginative and involved – I want to be all the things present governmental trends inhibit.

And then there is what I call the dimension of tenderness. It is that vital responsibility of government to demonstrate compassion for the needy and assistance for the disadvantaged, the equalization of opportunity for all, and an elevated sense of social responsibility that must continue to find favour with every thoughtful Canadian. Of all the challenges of government, no cause is more noble, no obligation more sacred. We shall be judged both as individuals and as a society by the manner in which we care for those unable to care for themselves.

So, who are these widget-makers? Well, they are you and me and people we have not even met. They are called Stelco and Northern Telecom; Mitel and Lavalin; M. Loeb and Campeau Corporation. They are called Nate's Delicatessen and Nabu and Blue Line Taxi Cabs. They are called the Steelworkers, the UAW, and the CNTU.

There are no fancy-pants heroes anymore with elegant theories and magic wands. There are only overworked and harassed businessmen and labour leaders and ordinary Canadians who get their hands dirty every day dealing with the pedestrian problems of providing jobs, meeting a payroll, and producing a product – only to come home at night to learn on TV that some brave new social artist has invented another government plan that will add to costs, increase paperwork, and lessen competitiveness.

As far as the great European, Pacific rim, or American markets are concerned, we are all widget-makers together. This may offend some Canadians, but these customers are not impressed with the cut of our jib or the colour of our flag. They are impressed with low-cost, high-quality, reliably delivered widgets.

If we come together in a national commitment to productivity enhancement to ensure their production – in a hundred different fields, from engineering to high tech to medical research, from flat steel to pens and pencils – we are in business: good, solid, profitable, ongoing business. If not, our children will never know how fulfilling it might have been.

Let me illustrate by discussing automobiles. Low-grade crude ore is mined in Labrador West and beneficiated into high-grade concentrate. It is moved 266 miles by train to Sept-Iles. Half the cargo moves 750 miles down river to Hamilton where it is made into steel, and then to Oshawa where a Chevrolet Cavalier is produced. The automobile is then shipped back to Labrador West where it is sold for $7,910.29, exclusive of Newfoundland sales tax.

The other half of the concentrate is moved 14,800 miles by sea to Japan where the same process unfolds and a comparable car – a Toyota Corolla – is produced. It is returned 14,800 miles by ship, moved up the railway, and sold in Labrador City for $7,358 – $552.29 less than its Canadian competitor. Moreover, this difference is after a GM rebate of $562.50. Were the temporary rebate not in effect, the price differential in Toyota's favour would be $1,131.68. (This information is based on actual quotes received by the Iron Ore Company of Canada for these products on March 25, 1982.)

The Japanese approach has three main objectives: keeping inventory to an absolute minimum; making sure that each step of the manufacturing process is done correctly the first time, even though the assembly line runs slower as a result; and continually reducing the amount of human labour that goes into each car.

And what are the results? They are shown on the accompanying table. Consider the indicators of all Japanese automobile companies combined, compared with their American counterparts, as analysed by the *New York Times*. The Japanese believe that of all the factors that affect productivity, people – their motivation, security, and reward – are the most important. They spare no effort or investment to produce generations of talented, sensitive, and responsive managers. Improved management development is a constant objective.

Comparison of Japanese and U.S. Automaking		
Average Automobile Plant	*Japan*	*U.S.*
Plant Personnel		
Total work force	2,360	4,250
Average number of employees absent	185	500
(vacations, illness, etc.)		
Manufacturing		
Parts stamped per hour	550	325
Time required to change dies	5 min.	4-6 hrs.
Time required to build a small car	30.8 hrs.	59.9 hrs.

CANADIAN MENNONITE BIBLE COLLEGE
LIBRARY   15
600 SHAFTESBURY BLVD.
WINNIPEG, MANITOBA R3P 0M4

Given this attitude, there should be little surprise that, in 1981, Toyota alone received 1.3 million suggestions—an average of twenty-seven from each company employee—designed to improve profitability, which in the last six months of that year helped cut costs by more than $45 million. A study by James E. Harbour indicated that between 80 per cent and 85 per cent of the Toyotas coming off the assembly line had no defects at all. At Ford, cars averaged seven or eight defects each. So what does all this mean?

On March 29, 1982, the following story appeared in the *Toronto Star*: "General Motors of Canada has lost a $100 million contract to sell cars to Iraq. Federal officials were informed yesterday by the Iraqi government that the huge deal has been cancelled because a previous shipment of Chevrolet Malibus was riddled with defective models. The Iraqis have now withdrawn their order for a further 12,500 cars, preferring to buy Toyotas from Japan instead."

So the Japanese spread their wings a little farther—this time to a rich new market in the Middle East. Canada has closed another door to its products. Meanwhile, the Japanese share of Canadian auto sales as a percentage of total has increased from 12.2 per cent in 1977 to 21.8 per cent in 1981. These figures track their productivity improvements and our decline almost to the penny.

It is evident that the productivity of the auto industry is important for all of Canada, but especially so for Ontario. As auto-industry expert Roy Wilson has pointed out, "Autos and parts account for 43 per cent of all the manufactured goods exported from the province." These are sobering numbers. In a real way they impact upon the economic well-being of every person in the country. This is not intended as an indictment of the Canadian automobile industry. I cite it—with sadness and regret—as a reflection upon all of us.

This one illustration regarding the automobile industry could apply to many companies in most of our industries. I know what it means to us, as Canadians, in human and economic terms. I know, too, what it means to the Japanese in terms of employment, favourable trade balances, a stronger currency, and lower inflation. And it can be traced right back to the widget—the Japanese widget, this time—low-cost, high-quality, reliably delivered widgets. They spell productivity. And that kind of productivity spells economic renewal.

So what can we do?

I do not claim the final word in this field but I offer the following thoughts.

1. Canada should proceed immediately to the creation of a national, tripartite Productivity Commission, composed of labour, management, and government.

2. The principal immediate objectives should be an agreement on a fair manner in which productivity increases can be measured, according to industry sector.

3. A national information program should be launched to educate the participants on the fairness and indispensability of such productivity-enhancement programs. The "straight goods" must be communicated to the individual worker. And he must know and be convinced that his restraint will be matched with restraint by other workers.

When I contemplate the hundreds of millions of dollars wasted annually by the federal government in self-serving advertising campaigns of every conceivable nature, it seems to me this is one program where the advertising dollar would be considered well spent.

4. The Productivity Commission should examine and recommend to the Minister of Finance substantial and desirable changes in the tax structure on a regular basis, prior to the preparation of the annual budget, to ensure that measurable improvements in productivity are rewarded. This is the carrot that will make things happen for all those who contribute to it – investors, management, and employees.

5. "Productivity bargaining" should be established in certain sectors as models to be followed, analysed, and improved upon by growing use elsewhere. The recommendation by Michael Warren, president of Canada Post Corporation, that such a dimension should be introduced into future collective bargaining talks is an excellent initiative and should be vigorously pursued, irrespective of the rather peremptory rejection of the concept by Jean-Claude Parrot. As president of the Canadian Union of Public Employees, Mr. Parrot, as well as other union leaders, knows full well that real wage increases cannot exceed the rate of growth of productivity. If wage settlements are higher, inflation will simply raise prices to eliminate the difference.

6. Beginning with the politicians and senior public servants, it should become a priority to reduce and eventually eliminate and outlaw indexed contracts and benefits, including indexed pensions, in line with a decline in inflation. Clear and justified exceptions should be made for mothers' allowances and all other social programs designed to protect the ordinary or disadvantaged Canadians from the ravages of inflation for which they are not responsible.

The phenomenon of rising expectations can only be broken by unquestioned personal example. The credibility of our elected leaders would be greatly enhanced in the eyes of the ordinary worker if he knew his leaders were bleeding a little bit themselves. I favour good, even handsome, retirement benefits for our elected representatives, who often serve at considerable personal sacrifice and family disruption. One can see, however, where this "indexed" road has led one province. My comments in this area deal principally with what has gone on in Quebec.

Collective bargaining in the province involves 250,000 public and para-public workers. How can one expect a leader such as Louis Laberge to respond seriously to requests for productivity-enhancement programs when legislators can retire after two elections and five years' service in the National Assembly with fully indexed pensions which can reach $25,000 a year payable immediately. These can rise to 30, 40, and 50,000 dollars a year and, believe it or not, can be received while the retired legislator is getting a larger amount from another provincial government job to which he was assured he would be appointed, prior to his retirement. In fact, Gilles Baril, the PQ Member for Rouyn-Noranda Témiscamingue, will be eligible to retire in 1986, if he wins his second election. He will then begin drawing this indexed pension for life. He will have reached the ripe old age of twenty-six.

No one has ever looted the public treasury with more elegant abandon. This is more money than most Canadians will see in a lifetime. The psychological barrier to progress in this area must now be dismantled by those who erected it in the first place. "The inflationary experience in the past decade," warns the Howe Institute, "has also created a situation in which people behave in anticipation of what they expect the future to hold – that is, higher inflation – thereby contributing precisely to that eventuality." It is unlikely that ordinary Canadians will take seriously warnings about the grave consequences of the social malady of indexing from those who have used their positions to shelter themselves from its effects.

7. Doing away with indexed pensions and benefits would produce a desirable result. According to Dr. Lester Thurow, a professor and consultant at MIT, without indexed contracts "nobody would sign a three-year contract." This may not be such a bad thing at all. All contracts in a given sector – such as the public sector in Quebec today – would expire at the same time. The Japanese call this "the spring offensive." According to Professor Thurow, "If every worker, union and non-union, had his wages set at the same time, it would be possible to have a national period of self-education about the economic facts of life. In a context where everybody would know what the other was getting, it might be possible to engineer a simultaneous slowdown in money wage increases so that they can come back into line with productivity gains." "Whipsawing," that familiar and dismal offshot of the present system, could become a casualty, and this would be good news for the entire country.

8. There must be a national commitment to civilizing labour relations in Canada. The adversarial system of labour relations ultimately produces just that – adversaries. It is rooted in a lack of proper two-way communication and results, inevitably, in mutual ignorance, hostility, and mistrust.

According to information from the Department of Labour, there has been since the 1960s a 600-per-cent increase in the number of days lost annually because of labour unrest. We can expect each year to lose between eight and ten million days for this same reason, without factoring in the enormous losses resulting from absenteeism and the like.

Some Canadians have achieved both prominence and affluence by ensuring that this sad state of affairs remains unchanged. Confrontation is their stock-in-trade. They have a vested interest in its continuation. The system itself needs to be made more responsive to our requirements.

As one who has worked as a labourer and truck driver, and whose father was a unionized electrician, I can tell you there is no substitute for treating workers with dignity at all times. There are dozens of ideas one can use to encourage this feeling. Success of quality-of-life programs depends on the acceptance by management that productivity cannot be the sole focus of initiatives. Good work environment and employee job satisfaction must be key objectives as well. Canadian employers must be encouraged to go the extra mile to avoid hurtful confrontations – and this does not mean giving away the store – which affect morale, productivity, and profits. Having done this, they will soon see movement on the other side.

9. In most Canadian operations, new labour-saving techniques result in layoffs. Professor Thurow has asked the right question: "Who is going to co-operate in raising productivity when it means the unemployment of either themselves or their friends?" Higher productivity ultimately leads to higher wages, but the *quid pro quo* has to be made obvious and desirable.

Canada is not Japan. We are different in many, many ways. But Canadian industry must begin, in a thoughtful and progressive manner, to devise programs based on Japan's employment guarantee, industrial lifetime tenure, productivity bonuses, seniority salary differentials, job enrichment or job rotation programs within work teams, ongoing employee retraining programs, and relocation assistance if it is to convince the Canadian workers they have much to gain when productivity rises. Our challenge in this area is to ensure that the burden of the costs of adjustment does not fall on the displaced worker alone.

10. The quest for an industrial strategy involves many important considerations, and all of them have their pros and cons. But our basic thrust must be to change and renew the structure of the Canadian economy in order to encourage growth. How should we do this? In my judgement, John Shepherd, former vice-chairman of the Science Council of Canada, expressed it best of all: "In an environment where losers are financed and winners are ignored, the vital entrepreneurial quality of our society is being suffocated. It is the task of industrial policy to reverse this process and to engineer an industrial future based on technological excellence and specialization. As a nation we have to become a winner with a risk-taking ethic."

Chapter II
Civilizing Labour Relations

When one looks at the international market for iron ore, with its strengths and weaknesses, it is tempting to conjure up the ideal setting, production facilities, and product that would enable us to meet world requirements on an uninterrupted basis.

The climate in Labrador West is far from hospitable – rainy summers and freezing winters are unfortunately the norm. Our reserves at Labrador City have an iron content of 38 per cent. Iron ore of this grade is not marketable and must be enriched, or beneficiated. Consequently, we have had to spend $600 million on the plant and facilities required to raise the iron content of our ore to 66 per cent, which is a marketable product. The region is isolated both from central Canada and the island of Newfoundland and complete training programs had to be instituted to provide the necessary expertise to operate the facilities. That, in a few words, is our situation.

If we had our druthers, what would the ideal situation be? Well, first of all, give us reserves of 1.5 billion metric tons with an iron content of 64 per cent, almost double that of our present grade. No costs would be required for beneficiation, the product having already been enriched by nature in the ground. Then, I would take proximity to a major city – say ten or fifteen miles from a metropolis of two million people with universities, trade schools, cultural centres, entertainment and sports facilities, all within easy reach of our employees. My ideal spot would have an annual temperature of approximately 75° F. and I would like a four-lane highway to provide access for our employees to every centre in the country. Obviously, we would need subsidized rail transport as well as a deep-sea port to ensure year-round shipping. Now, to round out my ideal, I would take cheap hydro power, accelerated depreciation, a ten-year income-tax holiday, and no labour problems. That ideal is no ideal at all. It is our competition – Brazil.

The viability of present iron ore operations in this province and the prospect of expansion or further development in Labrador West are tied directly to the ability to sell the product in direct competition with companies operating with the above advantages. To deliberately understate the case, our task is not an easy one.

Some people imagine that iron ore producers here have a real bonanza. Nothing could be further from the truth. In June of 1979, the Iron Ore Company of Canada, for example, paid a modest dividend to its shareholders. The last such dividend was paid in 1971, nine years earlier. Now how long would anyone retain an investment in a company with that kind of track record? I suspect not very long.

It seems to me that each time we feel we are on the verge of a major customer breakthrough, be it with China, Japan, eastern Europe, or elsewhere, the richly blessed and heavily government-assisted Brazilians are there, whipsawing cheaper prices. The competition is there and will, if anything, intensify in the future. So, all of us – management, employees, unions, and government – are faced with clear alternatives. We can either throw in the towel or strive to sharpen and enhance every available advantage to meet competition head on. Inasmuch as no reasonable person would long entertain the first option, we must redouble our efforts to ensure the viability of the second.

Our collective commitment must be to a dramatic improvement in productivity. According to every survey, Canada's productivity stacks up unfavourably against that of our competition. A recent U.S. Bureau of Labour Statistics study of productivity growth in twelve Western industrial nations indicated that Canada was almost at the bottom of the totem pole in gains. In fact, we were second to last, and you cannot do much worse than that. The highest rate – 12.9 per cent – was achieved in Japan and the lowest – 0.3 per cent – was in Sweden. Moreover, according to other figures, we are rapidly losing ground in direct economic terms. In per-capita production, we used to be Number Two in the world, second only to the United States. Now we have dropped to Number Twelve among the twenty-four countries that make up the Organization for Economic Co-operation and Development.

Each year, the OECD calculates the gross domestic product of each member country in U.S. dollars. This is then divided by the population of each, to give a direct measure of per-capita output. In 1979, Canada's per-capita output in U.S. dollars was $9,580. We were behind Switzerland, Denmark, Sweden, Germany, Luxembourg, Norway, Belgium, Iceland, France, the United States, and the Netherlands. The widening gap in these indicators jeopardizes our competitive position. We cannot expect or wish that the dollar remain substantially below par forever. Put more simply, low productivity leads to a lower standard of living.

One of North America's leading economists, John Kendrick of George Washington University, has put the case very clearly: "It is truly a vicious circle. Lower productivity has added to inflation. Inflation has reduced profits and reduced profits have further lowered investments and productivity."

Productivity measured as real domestic product per person employed has increased in the mining sector. The Economic Council of Canada points out that from 1948 to 1970, the pace of productivity advance was nearly 5 per cent annually, compared with 2.6 per cent for the entire economy. But as the C.D. Howe Institute indicated quite accurately: "Much of this productivity growth is, of course, attributable to the enormous capital inputs." (Net capital stock per worker in constant 1961 dollars expanded from $10,346 to $77,812 – a sevenfold increase – between 1966 and 1976.) The Howe study concluded that "total factor productivity, or the increase in output per unit of labour or capital combined, has actually been diminishing for metal mines since the beginning of the 1960s and for non-metallic mines since a peak in 1965."

In a sustained way, we must deploy every effort to improve our productive capacity, failing which we are clearly on a treadmill to oblivion. This includes ongoing capital expenditures, retraining initiatives, communications, and work enhancement programs by the company. It means profound attitudinal changes by management. It includes the elimination of the Pavlovian propensity by some government officials and agencies to believe that companies are there to be harassed and harangued rather than nurtured and encouraged. It includes an acceptance by the union leadership that innovative changes are not surreptitious threats to their members' welfare but responses to dynamic competition which, if left unchallenged, will dominate and eventually eliminate us from the picture altogether.

I discussed some of the natural advantages of our competitors. We are not, however, without resources ourselves, and these must be considered by prospective ore purchasers in any long-term arrangements:

1. We operate in the most politically stable climate in the world. When individuals or companies contemplate a billion-dollar investment, they want political stability above all else.

2. We have developed over two decades a highly skilled work force in Labrador which is 91 per cent indigenous. Our employees reside in excellent homes in a community where schools and attendant facilities, notwithstanding remoteness and climatic inclemency, rank with the best in Canada. The remuneration package of our employees is outstanding – more generous, in fact, than in any other mining location in the world. Modern telecommunications and jet travel have contributed to a mitigation of the isolation factor. It is still real, but, as the second generation of Labradorians enters the work force and voluntarily chooses to live and work there, it is slowly becoming "home."

3. Our known ore reserves are of reasonable quality and at present production rates have one hundred years' duration. They are all relatively contiguous to our ongoing mining and production facilities.

4. The present tax policy of the provincial government is a fair one and, when combined with the availability of hydroelectric power at reasonable rates, provides an important incentive to investors to continue and, hopefully, expand operations within the province.

5. Our management is young, adaptable, and responsive to challenge. For instance, the dramatic improvement in our labour-relations climate these last four years is a tribute both to their maturity and to the growing sense of reasonableness within the union leadership. Our objective is nothing less than the total elimination of the adversary relationship in the labour-management process. The following excerpt from the Quebec City newspaper Le Soleil appeared on January 22, 1981:

24

At the time of the last iron ore negotiation, the leaders of the United Steelworkers were "double crossed" by a handful of particularly active and aggressive union militants.

Thus, on March 9, 1978, around 4:00 a.m., the latter blocked the entrance gates to the Iron Ore Company and started a long and costly labour conflict, catching off guard the whole Sept-Iles population, their colleagues, and their own union leaders who had planned a coordination meeting for that day, to decide on the means to be used to accelerate the current negotiations.

This information was confirmed by Mr. Lawrence Mc-Brearty, Regional Coordinator for the United Steelworkers, as he was participating yesterday in an "open line" program on the local station CKCN. It was the first time that a union leader had, in fact, acknowledged the truth publicly.

You will recall that this walkout had rapidly spread to Wabush Mines, Quebec Cartier, and Sidbec-Normines, and involved some 10,000 steelworkers in Quebec and Labrador....

The repetition this year of the March 1978 scenario is a source of anxiety for the population of Sept-Iles and even more so for the management of the Iron Ore Company. Management has already pointed its finger at those responsible for the launching of the 1978 strike: a small "gang" of Marxists-Leninists working within Local 5569 and led by Mr. Gilles Lortie. Incidentally, the latter was present at the coordination table of the Steelworkers which met last week.

Thus, irrespective of the reason, the damage was done. We endured a four-and-one-half month strike and, in the process, lost $75 million. Immediately thereafter, in the summer of 1978, we created a Long-Range Corporate Planning Committee and, among other things, established our number-one objective as being the avoidance of all work stoppages through December 1981. This implied the successful renegotiation of all labour agreements. This objective has been achieved. We have now gone forty months without a work stoppage of any kind for any reason related to a labour-management problem. This might seem like small potatoes elsewhere, but it represents a milestone for us because it has never happened before in the recent history of the company.

To illustrate the importance of this new development and its impact upon the profitability of IOC, let me give you our consolidated net-profit figures after tax in Canadian dollars for the years 1977-1981, the period of my presidency of the Iron Ore Company of Canada:

1977	$ 46,983,000
1978	331,000
1979	109,381,000
1980	94,391,000
1981	123,940,000

Beginning in 1979, we started to show a return on assets of reasonable proportions, reaching approximately 10 per cent in 1981, hardly an abusive amount. The bad year, 1978, with its labour situation brought about by a handful of professional troublemakers and avowed Marxist-Leninists, sticks out like a sore thumb. So what did we do? What happened to dramatically alter our results?

We did not discover any richer ore. We did not discover cheaper power. We did not discover new markets, more inexpensive fuel, or lower shipping rates. We did discover that in the 1980s no one works *for* you any more. He either works *with* you or he does not work at all. We discovered that equipment does not make any money. The people who operate the equipment do.

We discovered that hours spent by top management at production meetings are of little value unless they spend many more hours concerning themselves with the problems of the people whose jobs and lives will be affected in consequence. Of all the factors that affect productivity, there can be no doubt that people are the most important. We discovered, strange to say, that people respond better to a "thank you" than they do to a kick in the butt. Simply put, we discovered that we are all alike – management, clerical, and unionized people; we want to be treated fairly; we do not like being humiliated; we want to have a say in how the job is to be run; we want to be respected and treated with dignity.

We also dealt head on with the cancerous issue of the Marxist-Leninists in Sept-Iles and their debilitating influence on our work force. Their avowed objective was to cripple employers on the

North Shore to prove their theory that the free enterprise system does not work. They had been largely responsible for the tragic social climate there throughout the 1970s.

In a major speech in Sept-Iles on November 9, 1980, I identified them publicly and invited our workers and the local population to examine their track record. I stated clearly that it was one of discord, disruption, and deceit. I indicated directly to our employees that they could no longer have it both ways—they could either believe the Marxist-Leninists or they could believe me, but not both. I am pleased to say that little has been heard from this small gang of rabble since. Their influence has evaporated and their record of strife and obstruction has been halted by the overwhelming majority of our employees who prefer the new course we are following.

For us, 1978 was not an isolated incident. In the previous decade, there had been three instances where the total work force was out on strike for an extended period of time, namely 8 per cent of 120 months. Moreover, there were fifty-two separate work stoppages, which ranged in duration from one hour to two weeks and affected from ten employees to 2,000. We have conservatively estimated this effect on our production to have been 2 per cent of the total force. This meant that in the ten years preceding July 1978, we had been shut down for one solid year.

When a company is faced with a heavy debt-repayment schedule, as a result of hundreds of millions of dollars in investment during this same period, it is indispensable that production be maintained in order that obligations be met to employees, shareholders, and lenders. It would be easy for me to say that the sole reason for our track record prior to 1978 was because we were called upon to deal with a truculent and irresponsible union. This, however, would not be true. Indeed, the real answer was more difficult and more complex than that.

To be sure, there were mitigating factors. For example, we are faced with fourteen different bargaining units associated with a number of different trade unions at Labrador City, Schefferville, Sept-Iles, Contrecoeur, and the Quebec North Shore and Labrador Railway, which is a wholly owned subsidiary. Moreover, we are confronted with the problem of operating in three different political jurisdictions and must, of course, on a daily basis, live with the

27

reality of two different language groups, almost equally distributed throughout these various jurisdictions. And so we concluded that our main problems resulted from a lack of a proper two-way communication, which inevitably results in mutual ignorance and mistrust.

In any case, the good and honourable attitudes I constantly detected at our board and executive committee levels were clearly not getting down through the ranks, nor were we receiving an accurate assessment of the employees' concerns and anxieties in return. In an era of such instantaneous communications, it seems rather unusual to make such an acknowledgement, but it was true.

The labour-relations record to which I have referred was costly for all of us. The loss in skilled workmen, high turnover rates, the concern among our clients about our reliability, cash-flow problems, the absence of dividends – all of these factors caused us to re-examine ourselves as managers and our approaches to problems and to attempt, in a spirit of firmness but coupled with a new degree of sensitivity to our employees' problems, to build a new and enduring era in labour relations at the Iron Ore Company of Canada.

We have referred to this attempt as a desire to eliminate "the strike syndrome." Our belief was that the adversary system of labour relations ultimately produces just that – adversaries. It was our intention – and we conveyed this view repeatedly and emphatically to both our union leaders and our employees directly – to go the extra mile to avoid hurtful confrontations throughout our system that inevitably affect morale, productivity, and, ultimately, profits.

And so we embarked on our program of communications and human-relations enhancement with some trepidation but no spirit of surrender. It was our intention to firmly and reasonably insist upon the respect of each and every provision of our fourteen collective agreements. We did, however, resolve to make every honourable human effort with our union leaders and our thousands of employees in an attempt to introduce a new degree of civility, of understanding, of genuine fraternity into our relations, which we believed would ultimately benefit all associated with the company.

A commitment to communications and improved human relations must be total. It must begin with the president and seep through all echelons of the company. It cannot be a one-shot deal. It is an ongoing process that must be maintained as the highest priority on a daily basis, 365 days a year.

All members of management must be committed to the concept. Attitudinal problems by some management officials have skewered more than one program less ambitious than our own. Management must be educated to the value of such a program, and if there is resistance by individual managers to the full and effective implementation of such an initiative, it must be dealt with firmly by the company president. As president, I will not allow any member of management to vitiate or circumvent our program in any way. In this area, we are not going back to the "good old days" because the "good old days" simply were not very good at all.

Our communications and human-relations program was open and constant. It extended to our employees, union leaders, government officials, communities in which we operate, and the public at large. Our finances, market projections, profits and losses, and capital-expenditure programs are now an open book. It is difficult to establish the value of such a program because ours was of necessity a learning experience for all concerned.

However, in 1981, this company, because of an unprecedented decline in world markets, suspended its operations at Sept-Iles and, in the process, laid off 1,000 workers. They all received handsome severance and retraining allowances, which were characterized by Angelo Forté, chairman of the Reclassification Committee appointed by the government of Quebec, as "among the most generous in Canadian industry." This action nevertheless took place during labour negotiations and in the middle of a Quebec provincial election campaign because we wanted this serious question to be dealt with "up front" by the parties. Some time later, we signed fourteen collective agreements covering all our employees at a cost well within accepted financial parameters. These difficult tasks were achieved with an absolute minimum of acrimony and in an atmosphere which would not have been conceivable three years earlier.

There is no magic in anything like this. And there is no "quick fix" for a bad situation, such as the one we had. The solution involves both the message and the messenger. If our employees came

29

to understand the former and respect the latter—as they did—it was because they perceived us to be in earnest, searching in good faith for a mutually acceptable method of operation in an increasingly competitive environment. (When we began to reach such basic financial objectives as had been clearly spelled out, the first thing we did was to share the profits directly with all employees and double the value of pensions being paid to the widows of deceased employees. This involved the outlay of several million dollars, and the impact of these gestures was immediate, dramatic, and overwhelmingly positive.)

Some of the items in such a program may strike one as basic, obvious, even trivial. And so they may be in isolation, one from the other. They include letters of appreciation to individual employees on a regular basis; lighted showcases at airports in Sept-Iles, Schefferville, Labrador City containing large colour displays honouring an employee, underlining his contribution to the company; a publicity program which, in a half-page ad each week in local and regional papers, honours an employee who has distinguished himself for his voluntary work on behalf of a recreational, sports, or cultural organization outside the company; twenty-fifth anniversary parties where we attempt to throw a first-class reception, dinner, and presentation of a substantial gift to each employee and his wife to indicate that we are most appreciative of their efforts and loyalty. We attempt, as well, given the difficulty in northern locations, to obtain qualified coaches for various organizations with the opportunity of obtaining expert instructors for training sessions. In these and dozens of other ways, we attempt, in a structured and ongoing manner, to recognize the indispensable contributions our employees have made to our survival and our success.

So, while such matters may seem small, a personal congratulatory note to an employee who was never thanked for anything in thirteen years with the company is not a small matter to him. The resolution of a housing problem in Labrador City is not insignificant to a man who feels he was treated with courtesy and fairness. The occasional public statement by the company president about the union's unprecedented contribution to a new degree of prosperity for all in difficult times does not fall upon deaf ears. But most of all it took time, the time and effort of a remarkably dedicated management team determined to make IOC a better place for all concerned.

I will not count the hours we spent in the mines, pellet plants, union meeting halls, and just plain social occasions with our employees and their union representatives discussing their problems, their perception of our mutual challenges, and their proposed solutions. I did not hestitate to act upon many of their suggestions, most of which substantially improved both the workplace and the atmosphere throughout the company. We began, as well, "brown bag" programs and quality of life circles designed to get unvarnished input from our employees.

Nor will I count the miles travelled by my senior colleagues and myself in pursuit of the objective that enhanced productivity begins with open dialogue and healthy labour relations. The results – dramatically different from those of the preceding ten years – are there for all to see. Our record to date has only made us realize how much more we have to do and how much better off our company will be if we persevere. There will be mistakes, disappointments, and problems in the future. But we know that these will be exceptions and that honourable solutions will emerge because of the people and programs we now have in place. The evidence is overwhelming that this new road we are travelling is a good one for IOC and all her people.

Chapter III
An Industrial Strategy

What I mean by an "industrial strategy" is a consensus worked out among the major economic partners—governments, management, and labour—to provide a framework within which to make economic policy and investment decisions. I stress the view that it must be a consensus. I reject any suggestion that a successful industrial strategy can be laid down from on high by government, like economic tablets of stone, and imposed on the private partners of our economy.

Many talk of industrial strategy in terms of picking "winners" and "losers." I buy half of that notion, at least in the sense of agreeing that part of the consensus has to be to identify national development areas, both geographic and sectoral, with the best growth potential. Part of the commitment from government has to be to target its positive support policies—whether through taxes, grants, or incentives—to those areas.

But I do not agree with those who would also spell out the "losers," beyond excluding some industries from the list of growth priorities, and thus from government-directed programs. Beyond that, I simply cannot accept that government—or anyone else—has a right to tell a businessman or woman and the employees that they are "losers" and, therefore, can no longer exist. I do not have that kind of faith in the wisdom of any group, particularly government; and frankly, it runs counter to my basic spirit of enterprise to tell people that they have no right to try to succeed in the business of their choice. Government can and should tell such Canadians that they are on their own in terms of support programs, but government should also add: "If you can make it on your own, more power to you."

It seems to me that, while it may not have been formalized into an industrial development framework, there already is, in fact, a considerable consensus among Canadians on the question of priority growth areas. We are, first and foremost, a resource-based economy, and that surely is the fundamental strength upon which we should be building in the final decades of the twentieth century. Not just energy, as important as that is, but also mining, forestry, agriculture, and fishing, too. And not just as extractors or primary producers of those resources, but as processors and manufacturers, and as suppliers of machinery and technology to our own resource industries. To those resource-based strengths, I would add communications and transportation – two areas in which we have developed great strength because the very nature of Canada has demanded strong communications and transportation – and high technology electronics, with special emphasis on technology relevant to resource, communications, and transportation development.

If we can reach a national consensus on that or some other list of priority growth areas for Canada, then it seems to me we will face three major requirements in translating that economic-development blueprint into an economic-development reality. First, we need co-operation; second, we need capital; and third, we need human resources. Let me examine each of them in turn.

When I look at Canada today, there is nothing I see that is more painful to me, as a citizen of one of the most blessed nations on earth, than the continual fighting and bitching that is going on among and between just about every major group in our society. One can hardly pick up a paper these days without finding one group of Canadians at the throat of another – Ottawa and the provinces, government and the business community, management and labour, teachers and school boards, doctors and health ministries. It is a continuous fight card in which it is difficult to find winners and easy to identify the loser – Canada itself. It seems the phrase "the common good" has been struck from our vocabulary.

We are all guilty of contributing to the bickering, even though we try to kid ourselves that we are the ones fighting for a "just" cause. But surely if there has been one perennial, main-bout contestant, it has been the Trudeau government. It has warred almost daily with the provinces, to the point where Prime Minister Trudeau pronounced the death-knell of co-operative federalism. Such tactics have destroyed any real relationship between government and industry, to the point where the overriding feeling toward Ottawa among business leaders is a combination of anger, distrust, and dismay. It has soured relationships with organized labour to the point where the two sides are not even talking to each other, except to unleash another volley of abuse.

There was a time, when we were younger and things were better, when many Canadians, I think, looked upon Trudeau's penchant for confrontation as a kind of political theatre. Well, we may still find that more than four hours of Napoleon-versus-Europe makes a good movie, but we know now that more than fourteen years of Mr. Trudeau-versus-everyone-else makes lousy government.

Our priority must be to restore civilized dialogue and discourse to the partnership of governments and to the relationship between the public and private sectors of the country. Without mutual respect and trust, there is only deadlock. The problems facing the country cannot be traceable in their entirety to the actions of any one individual. Yet let me suggest that any starting point has to be the removal from the national scene of a stumbling block like Mr. Trudeau. The process of reconciliation requires leadership from the top. The one thing that Trudeau has shown us clearly is that he cannot lead Canadians and bring them together into a consensus. Once we have restored some sense of co-operation among the partners in our economy, then we can turn our attention to the next major requirement, and that is the capital financing of Canada's national development to the year 2000.

The size of our future capital requirements is truly astounding. According to the government's task force on mega-projects, on major projects alone, before the end of the century, investments of almost $500 billion will be required. Other studies estimate total capital requirements for the 1980s at well over one trillion dollars. Such sums are so large they are hard to comprehend. In terms easier to grasp, such expenditures will require earmarking for capital investment more than twenty-five cents of every dollar of national wealth we generate during this period.

It is not surprising that the mega-projects are dying, when they are not, like the Alsands project, already dead. The deterioration in world markets for energy has made mega-projects less attractive financially. The federal government's last-minute offer to save Alsands was, by any reasonable standard, a generous one. But the problem was much deeper than that. The problem lies in the lack of confidence and trust brought about by the government's National Energy Program.

Were it not for the punitive, vexatious, and confiscatory provisions of the National Energy Program, there is no doubt but that Alsands and Cold Lake – with a $25-billion investment and thousands upon thousands of precious jobs – would be well underway today. Ours is a mixed economy, and the concept has produced many beneficial results for Canadians. But the motor of the mixed economy is the private sector. It must be kept running at all times.

The fate of Alsands is instructive. It could have worked, but it will only go ahead when there is in Ottawa a federal government committed to the private-enterprise system. A number of considerations brought about its demise, but two stand out. One, the cash flow of the companies involved was gravely impaired by the federal "tax grab" to pay for its own deficits. The federal action resembled nothing more than a hold-up at the corner gas station at 3:00 a.m. Two, there was so much retroactivity and confiscation in the NEP that major investors lost whatever trust and confidence they had in the government. They would no longer make long-term commitments because they no longer believed that the government would honour its own undertakings. Investors did not feel the government to be as good as its word. So they withdrew.

The challenge is clear. We must elect a new government, one that understands such matters, and get on with the business of building a nation. Let us start investing in our future instead of trying to buy back the past.

As we contemplate the sad state of this splendid nation, we search for reasons why things are as they are. One major reason is that we have a federal government committed to a social democratic-collectivist philosophy. There is no room in its vocabulary for words like risk, sacrifice, reward, initiative, enterprise, and profit.

Given the courage of our people and our remarkable resource base, we can still meet the astronomical targets for mega-projects and related developments, provided governments get their financial act together and stop draining away the savings of individual Canadians and corporations, as they did during the 1970s, to finance their deficits; provided we are prepared to be a bit more sensible and realistic in our attitude toward foreign investment; provided Canadian corporations are prepared to stop investing so much of the country's scarce resources in the unproductive game of corporate takeovers. I have yet to see a takeover that has created a single job – except, of course, for lawyers and accountants.

Another major requirement, if we are going to achieve this country's development potential in the 1980s, is to ensure that we have the human resources necessary to develop and manage our own economy. It is truly shocking that when we have more than one million Canadians out of work we still have to import skilled tradesmen from outside Canada. And yet that is precisely what we are doing. Employment Minister Lloyd Axworthy has admitted we are looking for 25,000 immigrants to fill skilled-trades openings in Canada. The C.D. Howe Institute has estimated that by 1985 we will be short 30,000 skilled workers in the so-called "blue-collar" trades alone.

To understate the case, these are appalling facts. What does it say about our planning, objectives, and manpower-training and relocation programs? At a time when educators at all levels are demanding that governments continue to fund our education system at higher levels, surely it is not unfair to ask, in return, for some assurance that our sons and daughters will come out of that system with the skills and training they need to find satisfying, permanent jobs. Perhaps it is not asking too much, either, for governments to take up one of the rare joint initiatives of labour and management – the proposals made by the Canadian Labour Congress and the Business Council on National Issues for a massively improved program of on-the-job or apprentice training by Canadian companies to ensure that our young people need no longer fear closed doors and bleak futures.

By no means is this a definitive statement on industrial strategy. Obviously, a complete national development program has to come to grips with our sorry record in research-and-development spending, and with our inadequate export support programs, to name but two other factors. Yet even so, the three main components of an industrial strategy should be apparent to all.

First, we require co-operation to re-establish the concept of working together as Canadians first—the concept around which this nation was built.

Second, we must make an effort to ensure that we have the capital required to finance national development in the 1980s, including a commitment from all sides to avoid the kind of vexatious and punitive policies that serve only to drive away Canadian and foreign capital.

Third, we need a major national program to train and retrain the richest resource of all—our people—so that all Canadians may share in our development by working and by paying our own way.

Chapter IV
Research and Development

Euromoney, the leading economic journal from London, rates the performance of countries according to an accepted set of economic criteria. It published the results of an important analysis in October 1982. And where was Canada? Second? Tenth? Fourteenth in the world? On the basis of our economic performance between 1974 and 1982, Canada landed in fortieth place.

Our great weakness was poor economic growth. We ranked fiftieth in economic growth in the last eight or so years. How the mighty and the generously endowed have fallen!

Let me illustrate a part of the problem. According to a study made by the National Energy Board, *Pipeline Construction Costs: 1975-1985*, future energy mega-projects could be endangered because of the following facts:

- Pipeline costs are $1 million a kilometre, and they rose faster than the inflation rate for the past six years.
- Since 1975, labour charges on pipeline construction have nearly doubled, and in 1981 alone were up 25.9 per cent.
- Salaries, including benefits, for Canadian pipeline welders rose by 44 per cent in 1981 to $3,046 a week. U.S. pipeline welders get $1,665 a week.
- Canadian welders earn productivity bonuses – a practice discontinued in the U.S. – which are normally paid as four hours a day at double time, about $1,030 a week.
- Despite higher wages, pipeline contractors say productivity has declined.

We seem to have lost our competitive edge. Our collective inclination, after fifteen years of a Trudeau government, seems to be acceptance of a lesser status. Our will to excel as a people has been gravely sapped.

How can we pull through?

The starting line for me is the technological dimension. Either we go into the game and become important players in this major league or we become a nation that will, during its entire lifetime, play in the Junior B circuit. To play with the majors, we must make a firm commitment to double the public and private funds allocated to research and development before 1985. Research and development, and the resulting innovations, are the lifeblood of a successful economy and country.

The importance of increased investment in research and development in designing an industrial strategy is overwhelmingly clear. In 1968, however, when Pierre Elliott Trudeau became Prime Minister, we were spending 1.4 per cent of the gross national product in this vital job-productive area. For a decade we spent only 0.9 per cent, and in the last two years we have spent 1.13 per cent. So now, a decade and a half later, the Trudeau government has the nerve to announce a new objective: 1.5 per cent. This illustrates how our national government is illogical and how it lacks an earnest commitment toward this cornerstone of our economy.

As a percentage of its population, Canada employs in research and development one-third as many people as do the Swedes, the Germans, and the Japanese, and one-half as many as the Dutch, the French, and the Americans. Of all the industrialized countries of the Western world, Ireland and Iceland are the only countries that invest less than we do in this vital field. Only 21,519 Canadians are working in the field of industrial research and development. One company alone in West Germany, Siemens, with its 30,000 employees in industrial research and development, possesses 42 per cent more researchers than Canada as a whole. One American company alone, IBM, spends more annually for research and development than Canada. In the course of the last ten years, 94 per cent of all patents granted by Canada were granted to foreigners.

These other countries, even the smallest among them, have realized that in a new era technology represents power. As Walter Light of Northern Telecom said: "Technology is like oil. You cannot do without it. If you do not have it, you must buy it from those who possess it. And like oil, you must buy it at their price. However, contrary to oil, you can create technology. It is one of the rare resources which is inexhaustible." This is the great challenge which must be faced in the next quarter century. We must be in the game in the major leagues, and not in Junior B where successive Liberal governments have placed us.

It is important that the federal restraint program of 6 and 5 not be applied to research and development. The National Research Council, which acts as Canada's main research laboratory, needs a funding increase of at least 20 per cent to bring it up to approximately $400 million. The Council is midway through year two of a five-year plan to assist Canada's high-tech manufacturing sector in doubling its productivity and exports over the next decade.

In the past year, Sweden, Japan, and France have announced higher goals for R & D spending. OECD figures indicate that of the eighteen major industrialized nations, Canada ranks twelfth in gross expenditures on R & D. This is not good enough, not by a long shot, because, as Don McGillivray, economics editor for Southam Press, has pointed out, "Even if Canada does reach the goal of 1.5 per cent of GNP by 1985, we will still lag behind other countries ... in fact if the U.S. effort were to stand still, as of today, American R & D spending will be fourteen times Canada's."

The governments of these other countries have understood – whereas the Canadian government refuses to understand – that the jobs of tomorrow, the pursuit of their high standard of living, the health of their economy, depend on the success or the failure of their technologies and of their capacity to create them and to develop them more rapidly and more cleverly than other countries.

The government of Quebec has understood this need. Bernard Landry in his volume *Building Quebec II* expressed these sentiments. In Quebec there is everything it takes to become a nerve centre in the field of R&D: universities, qualified manpower, research centres, social infrastructure, etc. The only thing missing is the desire of the federal government to set objectives that correspond to the demands of the situation and the talents of our people and to act with Quebec in order that these objectives may become a reality.

The Prime Minister has established his credentials as one who prefers to curse the darkness rather than "light a candle." He announced that co-operative federalism is dead. As the chief hatchet man, he should take little pride in such a statement, particularly inasmuch as such federalism is dead only in his mind. Let him now work with Quebec to disprove his own assertions. Let him use his power to create a unique climate within which a rush to excellence will begin in the field of research and development that will excite and challenge and reward our youth. And what wealth, what magnificent opportunities will be derived therefrom for an entire generation of our youth who do not ask for anything more than to be employed in productive and stimulating jobs in their own province or country. In fact, if the percentage of GNP allocated to research and development were increased by 1 per cent, we could create in Canada one million new jobs and $20 billion in additional sales of manufactured products.

We have an urgent need at the present time for a dramatic and innovative fiscal reform in regard to investments in high technology. We must formulate a fiscal formula which will incite not only already important companies but also thousands and thousands of small and medium investors to forge ahead and become the owners of this new generation of companies, and in so doing to create hundreds of thousands of new jobs.

If this country can afford to give total write-offs on third-rate motion pictures that no one would want to show even in his basement, we can certainly do no less for high-tech investments that will ensure a viable future for our children.

In presenting a long-range plan for a dramatically escalated commitment to research and development, Dr. Larkin Kerwin, president of the National Research Council, a public servant who understands the problems of the real world and the frustrations that go with it, stated the problem and possibilities well:

If Canada implements something like this plan, it will still have problems in the years ahead. But these will be the problems of excellence – the worries of the rich. They will probably include a scarcity of workers rather than unemployment; a surplus of affordable energy, much of it in renewables; so strong a dollar, and so low a national debt, that we may be pressured, as Japan is now, to limit our exports. These are genuine difficulties and I

41

do not minimize them. But I would rather deal with them than with the stagnancy we face today.

Our challenge is clear. Without economic well-being, there is no foundation upon which nationhood can flourish. Together – government, business, labour, and education – we must raise our productive output to unprecedented heights. If we can base our industrial strategy as a nation soundly upon this principle, which includes the massive recycling of our manpower, we may yet recover those dreams of childhood and save a large part of Laurier's hope, in order to produce, together, a series of splendid accomplishments for Canada, unrivalled by any other nation in the industrialized world.

Chapter V
Control of Government Spending

Is there a Canadian who does not know too well the sad litany of federal government spending?

When Pierre Elliott Trudeau took office, we had a government in Ottawa that spent $10 billion a year. Today, we have a government in Ottawa that overspends by more than $18 billion a year, and the amount is escalating monthly. This is nearly double the U.S. deficit on a per-capita basis. We have a government whose annual interest charges on its debt now exceed $13 billion.

Perhaps worst of all, we have a spending system which two independent authorities, the Auditor General and the Lambert Commission, have told us is literally out of control. "The Government," said the Auditor General, "has lost or is close to losing effective control of the public purse."

This situation is cause for national concern in its own right. The government, after all, has no money – it spends our money – and thus we have every right to be deeply concerned about what Ottawa's spending policies mean in terms of direct impact on our welfare. That impact in itself is substantial enough. A study done by the Fraser Institute of Vancouver indicated that the average Canadian, in effect, now works half the year for the government; he only gets to see any real income for himself in the latter six months of the year.

So where does our money go?

- Central Mortgage and Housing Corporation (CMHC) bought the Quai D'Orsay Hotel in Ottawa for $3 million and resold it for $1 million. It bought the Howard Johnson's Hotel in Montreal for $19 million and sold it for $6 million.

- CMHC, as well, embarked on a land-banking program, lost $775 million in six years, and then abandoned the program as a total and spectacular failure.
- Canadian International Development Agency (CIDA) spent $1.4 million on a fisheries training vessel that was supposed to cost $308,000 to purchase and refit. The government of Columbia refused to accept the ship because it would not float.
- CN spent $64,244 to buy advertising space to wish CP a happy birthday.
- A study by the Auditor General found that work performed by 50,000 clerical and regulatory employees could have been done by 38,000. Employee efficiency was 60.8 per cent, compared with an acceptable minimum of 80 per cent and a private sector average of 87.7 per cent. Overruns totalling $1.1 billion have been produced. Twenty-one overruns alone cost $920 million.

Such waste is serious enough in itself. But even more serious are two problems raised by the continued profligate and wasteful spending of our federal government. The first problem is that when government allows its spending to get out of control, it wastes not only our money but its own credibility. It forfeits its own leadership role in terms of being able to mobilize public opinion and public action in the name of Canada's national interest. A national government unable to provide that kind of leadership is, in the end, a government unable to lead and unable to govern.

That, sadly – I say sadly because this is more than a partisan concern – is precisely the kind of government we have in Ottawa. At a time when we so desperately need leadership able and credible enough to mobilize our citizens to meet our current economic challenges, especially the challenge of bringing individual restraint to the fight against national inflation, the Trudeau government is literally unable to speak with the slightest degree of believability to the people of Canada.

How can a government call on a nation to restrain itself and to be more realistic in its collective demands upon our economy when its own record is an unbroken string of fiscal excess? Canadians may be many things, but stupid we are not. We simply will not buy leadership that so blatantly has one code of conduct for itself and quite a different one for the rest of us.

The second problem the Trudeau government has created by its excessive spending is to diminish gravely Ottawa's capacity to act as a stabilizing force within our national economy.

Most of us still believe that economic stabilization is a legitimate, even necessary, role of a national government. To put it in its simplest, Keynesian terms, public-sector investment and stimulus can help the economy through the troughs of the economic cycle when private economic expansion is temporarily slowed and depressed. But a government can play that stimulative role during an economic downturn only if it has some fiscal room for manoeuvre. And it can only have that room if it does not exhaust its financial capacity during relatively good economic times when there is no need – and no justification – for public stimulus of the economy.

Some commentators would have us believe that this elementary form of Keynesian economics just up and died one day. They are wrong. Keynesian economics has been smothered by the Trudeau government in one of the cruelest acts of economic infanticide in recorded history. Regardless of economic circumstance, regardless of economic need, despite any elementary rule of fiscal prudence, the government continued to spend and to spend and to spend – thereby destroying its own capacity to act as a vital stabilizing force in the Canadian economy. By any definition of Keynesian economics, the federal government should have had surpluses in three of the last five years.

How can the government stabilize anything when it builds up a $10-billion deficit before a recession? At a time with little or no economic growth and substantially more than one million Canadians out of work, when one could make a good case for government to help the economy through the recession, the Trudeau government is so broke from a decade and more of abusive spending that it cannot help anyone, least of all itself. It cannot stimulate the economy because it has exhausted all of its fiscal room for manoeuvre, all of its fiscal credibility, feeding its own endless appetite to grow and spend. And there it lies, like a beached whale, belly up, praying for a strong wave and a sunny day.

If those are two of our most pressing problems, what may be

offered by way of solution? Let me offer five ideas for consideration.

1. My starting point on the issue of government spending is freedom of information. We cannot even begin to come to grips with this problem unless and until the books of government are opened up so that we all can see what is being done with the cash. The key to accountability is information. Without complete and timely information, our parliamentarians are reduced to sleepwalking in the night.

Unlike the Liberals, the Conservatives can be proud of their effective freedom-of-information legislation, which was one of the earliest acts of the Conservative government. That piece of legislation should have been passed by the House immediately. All Canadians should regret that it was not passed into law in 1979, and every Liberal worthy of the name should have the decency to be embarrassed by the charade the Trudeau government has made of this basic principle of democracy.

The Trudeau government has proclaimed its commitment to the principle of freedom of information for a decade, and it has spent every minute of those ten years ensuring that no effective action was taken on the subject. The Liberals are eviscerating that legislation, the way a butcher plucks a chicken. By the time it is passed, there will be nothing left but the feathers.

2. If we are to regain control of federal spending, we must restore parliamentary accountability for government expenditure. Most of us grew up believing that a check on the King's purse was at the very heart of what Parliament was all about. Today, we have a check on nothing. Instead, we have a system where overly large parliamentary committees, deprived of expert permanent staff, are handed billions of dollars of expenditures to study, with an arbitrary deadline that requires that these expenditures be considered approved by a certain date. It is a sham and a disservice to the most fundamental idea of parliamentary supremacy.

That has to change. We need, at least for the examination of spending estimates, smaller committees or subcommittees able to take a manageable piece of the $60-billion spending empire and look at it thoroughly with the help of expert staff. We need to lift the artificial deadline on at least some of these estimates so that, if Parliament is dissatisfied with some major spending program, it has the clout with which to pressure the government for change.

3. We must ensure that there is public accountability of all Crown Corporations to Parliament. The more they proliferate, the more they gobble up huge chunks of tax dollars, the less accountable they become and the less relevant Parliament really is. Many of the people who run tax-financed empires would not recognize a bottom line if they tripped over one. They must be made directly responsible to our elected representatives for the handling of our money. And they must be subject to the same penalties and consequences as the rest of us, if they fail to produce with efficiency and economy.

4. We need sunset laws. When any new spending program or government agency is created, approval for it would carry an automatic rider requiring the program or agency to be resubmitted to Parliament for a fresh mandate within, say, five years. Unless it can justify its continued existence in some form, Parliament would let the sun set on it – and we, as taxpayers, might see an occasional ray of light.

5. But the federal government is only one of many governments in Canada. Its expenditures on goods and services are matched by those made by the provinces and matched again by the municipalities. A solution to financial management and accountability problems at the federal level is a solution to only one-third of the concerns of Canadian taxpayers. And, because of the number of governments in that other two-thirds, the solutions there may be more difficult to implement but are of no less importance.

I think it is time governments, particularly federal and provincial, took up the serious question of what my friend, former Ontario Treasurer Darcy McKeough, calls the "disentanglement" of federal and provincial spending programs. To put it mildly, there are simply far too many areas of activity where we are duplicating expenditure programs by the two sets of government. There is one big flaw in this system – there is only one set of taxpayers. And you and I end up paying twice for essentially the same service.

I am not referring here to constitutional amendments or major changes in the formal powers of any level of government. I am talking about a process of fiscal and administrative realism – the doctrine of common sense – on the part of our federal and provincial governments, based on the concept that efficiency and accountability demand an end to this costly overlap of services. But there will never be co-operation among partners when someone is dedicated to "confrontational federalism" – it just will not happen.

Those are five specific ideas on government spending, but basic to them is the need for a change of attitude. In private or corporate roles, we know we face one hard reality – we can go broke if we continuously spend more money than we earn. Governments, unfortunately, lack that essential discipline. They operate on the basis that there is no bottom to our pockets. Now they have finally hit rock bottom themselves.

This family shot was taken in our Montreal home. It shows my wife Mila and myself and our three children, Mark, Caroline, and Benedict.

Here I am, in the arms of my father Benedict Mulroney, outside the family house at Baie Comeau.

This is a photograph I treasure.
It was taken at the Leadership Convention
in 1956 when I was Vice-Chairman of the
National Youth for Diefenbaker Committee.

Quebec Premier Robert Bourassa (seated) accepts the massive report of the Cliche Commission, May 2, 1975. The three-member Commission consisted of (left to right) myself, Robert Cliche, and Guy Chevrette.

*The immense size and scale of the North Shore operations of the
Iron Ore Company of Canada must be seen to be appreciated. But some indication
of the scope of operations is apparent in these photographs.*

*Meeting with the people who work on the job site confirmed my
belief that it is not equipment that makes a company—or a country—prosperous.
It is the people who operate the equipment who do.*

Of all the factors that affect productivity, there can be no doubt that people are the most important.

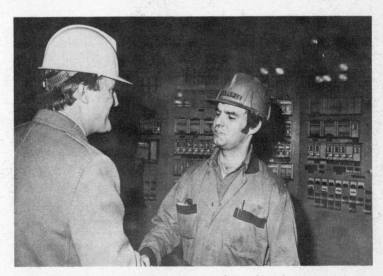

During my years at IOC, I committed myself and management to the importance of civilizing labour relations.

Here I am addressing a company function in 1980. The occasional public statement by the president about the union's unprecedented contribution to a new degree of prosperity for all in difficult times does not fall upon deaf ears.

*At the Iron Ore Company of Canada we instituted a
program of honouring employees who had distinguished themselves
for voluntary work on behalf of recreational, sports, or
cultural organizations outside the company.*

*Countless hours were spent in mines, pellet plants, union meeting halls,
and just plain social occasions with employees and their spouses.*

*An address to the Canadian Institute of
Mining and Metallurgy, St. John's, Newfoundland,
November 8, 1981.*

Chapter VI
Reforming the Budgetary Process

At a time when governments are supposedly committed to greater openness and accountability, the budget-making system remains cloaked in secrecy. At a time when virtually all other policy decisions are subject to an elaborate system of checks and balances within government and Parliament, the budget remains the exclusive prerogative of a handful of officials within the Department of Finance and the Privy Council Office.

In an age when we know that government works best when it builds a consensus of public understanding prior to taking formal action, the budget is "dropped out of nowhere" one night, with virtually no effort having been made to achieve agreement or even understanding of its principal goals. As Oliver Wendell Holmes once observed: "I find a great thing in this world is not so much where we stand as in what direction we are moving."

Where it is now routine for government legislation to be referred to a parliamentary committee for expert testimony, and to allow affected groups and individuals to comment, all budget bills – which are among the most important and complex measures the government introduces – continue to be dealt with by the full House of Commons sitting as a committee of the whole, where no experts and no interest groups can be heard.

No process in the world will prevent bad decision-making. But the present budget-making process itself contributes to bad decision-making and therefore to bad government. Clearly, it is time for a serious debate in Canada on how we can make the budget process more responsive and more effective to the benefit of all Canadians. I offer the following thoughts.

1. Why not agree that the budget will be brought down at rela-

tively the same time each year, perhaps during the final two weeks of November. That in itself would help demystify some of the process and do away with the annual cat-and-mouse game of Opposition MPs asking the Minister of Finance almost daily questions about a budget date. The other half of the government's fiscal program – the tabling of annual spending estimates – already is regularized in regard to timing and occurs late in February. A government, of course, can bring in economic measures at any time during the year. It loses no policy flexibility if it agrees that the budget – the full-blown presentation of national accounts and its major package of tax reforms – will be introduced in late November each year.

2. The first major purpose of a budget is to set the broad economic direction of our country. It follows that the national interest would be best served if we had as much debate and input as possible on what that direction should be before the budget is introduced. We could have that kind of public discussion of general economic goals by empowering the House of Commons Committee on Finance and Economic Affairs to hold formal, pre-budget hearings and issue a report to the government before the introduction of the budget.

Public policy discussion could only improve the budget process. Hearings and Commitee deliberations will not always produce agreement or even consensus, but they will at least ensure that the options are examined in public, in view of all Canadians. And the Committee's report would be a valuable working document for the government to consider in preparing the budget. If I were Minister of Finance, I would welcome such a pre-budget discussion on the grounds that the more Canadians understand about economic conditions, the more likely they would be to accept painful decisions deemed necessary for the long-term good of the country.

Perhaps the annual *Review of the Economic Council of Canada*, a valuable document that now receives virtually no formal consideration, could be referred to the Committee as a basic reference document. Senior government officials, the governor of the Bank of Canada, and major private organizations, representing business, labour, consumers, farmers, and others, would be invited to appear as witnesses, along with the senior officers of major economic research groups like the C.D. Howe Institute and the Fraser Institute. I should stress again that the debate would be limited to broad economic considerations; these hearings would not be a forum for any interest group to plead for detailed tax changes of interest and benefit to themselves.

3. A simple procedural suggestion concerns the question of accountability. One of the most objectionable aspects of the budget process is that budget measures usually take effect the moment they are announced. I believe it should be accepted as a matter of principle that no new budget measure takes effect until it is actually passed by Parliament and given Royal assent. Exceptions could be made for those measures having direct market consequences, tariff implications, and the like.

There is the counter-argument that the time-lag between announcing a new budget measure and actually putting it into effect could produce distortions in short-term economic activity. However, if one refers to past budgets, there are numerous measures which by their nature would not have provoked any type of distortion of economic activity. With respect to those measures that are likely to provoke distortions in short-term economic activity, the opportunity of keeping such measures secret should be weighed against the often more important principle that it is profoundly undemocratic for a government to begin to collect taxes simply on the basis of a speech by the Minister of Finance, before elected representatives have had any opportunity to scrutinize the Minister's proposals and offer amendments to them.

4. The second major purpose of a budget is to make specific changes in the tax system. There is a lot of criticism these days to the effect that tax reform is a kind of "ivory-tower" process in Ottawa, prepared by officials who are long on theories of equity and justice and short on practical knowledge of what specific tax changes will mean to companies and working Canadians. Certainly recent budgets have done nothing to discourage such criticism.

The problem may be largely one of methodology. The present budget-making process almost guarantees that tax changes will be proposed by politicians and government officials who do not like to admit publicly that they make mistakes and are working in the dark without adequate knowledge of what their provisions will mean in actual practice. The 1981 budget, for example, contained 218 separate tax changes affecting millions of taxpayers and amounted to a massive overhaul of the entire tax system.

To improve this budget purpose, a procedure similar to that in effect in Britain should be implemented. There the finance bill, which follows from the budget and incorporates the government's taxation proposals, is given detailed examination annually by a standing committee of the British House of Commons. A variation on this procedure should be considered for Canada. All technical tax changes should be introduced in the budget as a draft bill and, further, such a bill should be referred as a matter of automatic procedure to a subcommittee of the Committee of Finance and Economic Affairs for hearings and deliberations. Thereafter, the redrafted bill would be resubmitted to the full House of Commons for legislative action. The subcommittees would be supported by a permanent, highly skilled staff of economists, accountants, and lawyers specializing in tax law, and it would, of course, invite such leading groups as the Canadian Tax Foundation to provide the legislators with the benefit of their input and expertise.* That was in some measure the kind of process followed by then Finance Minister Edgar Benson when he introduced a major tax-reform package in the early 1970s. And the result surely was better tax laws—tax laws with more public understanding and support than have been won for the current measures being pushed through by a majority government.

*There are two matters that could be immediately referred to the proposed subcommittee of the Committee of Finance and Economic Affairs.

1. Eliminate the interest-deductibility provision on non-productive corporate takeovers in Canada to ensure that large pools of capital are not diverted to useless empire-building. Exceptions to this rule should be in those areas where jobs will be saved as a result of the takeover or where the job-creation component is high.

2. Allow municipalities to issue tax-free bonds, provided that the proceeds from the bonds are tied to capital projects designed to create employment and not to cover operating costs or municipal frills. By using this instrument, which has been a standard feature of U.S. tax law for many years, the federal government can, in fact, get twice as much clout for its contribution than it would in making direct grants. The jobs created by enhancing the social or economic infrastructure of the country are far more beneficial than the short-term artificial props we presently see in such efforts.

Certainly a system of draft tax legislation and subcommittee examination would mean it would take longer to get tax laws changed. It is quite predictable that Opposition members, in particular, would be tempted to use the process – at least in its initial stage – to delay action. But surely we could suffer a few weeks' delay in the name of better legislation.

5. The major support and background papers that provide the detailed rationale and evidence used by the Department of Finance to advance various policies should be made public. We would then know the principal basis of government policy. It would have the salutary effect of enhancing the quality of such papers if their authors knew they would be scrutinized by outsiders. Inasmuch as we are paying for this information, it does not seem unreasonable that we should have access to it. Freedom of information should apply to the Finance Department as well as to Veterans Affairs.

6. Specific matters that cannot properly be dealt with in isolation because of their widespread fiscal implications, such as interest deductibility and capital gains, should be referred to the Committee with a specific mandate to report back with a complete set of integrated proposals.

7. Sunset provisions should be attached to broad sectors of the Tax Code to ensure their statutory and periodic review by the Committee. Exceptions could be made to ensure that long-range financial commitments by investors are not unduly inhibited by such provisions.

8. Nominees for deputy-ministerial appointments to Finance and other economic ministries should be required to appear before the members of the Committee to explain their personal views on a broad range of economic, fiscal, and monetary matters that go to the very heart of their ultimate influence on the budget and, hence, our lives. It could be decided by the House whether the Committee should have a veto over such appointments, but in any event the background and competence of such nominees should be intensely scrutinized prior to their appointments taking effect.

No one has the final word on the subject of reforming the budget process. But everyone should remember that the government has no money of its own – it has our money. How it is used should interest every Canadian in a real way. All of us who are interested in parliamentary democracy and in good government should recognize the fact that the present budget-making process does not work. We may perversely take some enjoyment from the discomfort it causes Liberal Ministers of Finance, but surely none of us can take any comfort from the grave damage it is doing our country.

Chapter VII
Thoughts on the Constitution

1

Twenty years ago, when I attended law school, much of every working day was spent discussing the Constitution. Twenty years later, a lot of people still do precisely the same thing – and in the intervening period, not a single comma has been changed in the BNA Act.

While I attended Université Laval, the students founded the Congress of Canadian Affairs, a symposium that was an offshoot of Quebec's Quiet Revolution. It devoted its time to an analysis of federal-provincial relations. In the 1960s there were, apart from non-stop conferences at the provincial governmental level, the Laurendeau-Dunton Commission, the Pépin-Robarts Commission, and more white papers, green papers, and beige papers than you can shake a stick at.

Among the organizers of that Congress were: Pierre de Bané, Clément Richard, Denis de Belleval, Michel Cogger, Lucien Bouchard, André Ouellet, Michael Meighen, Jean Garon, and Peter White. It was evident that, within the organization committee itself, there was matter for debate. Among the guest speakers were Jean Lesage, Davie Fulton, Mason Wade, Marcel Chaput, Jean-Jacques Bertrand, Maurice Lamontagne, René Lévesque, Douglas Fisher, André Laurendeau, and Daniel Johnson.

I was chairman of a panel discussion that made national headlines. On the panel was Marcel Chaput, the Quebec civil servant who worked for the Ministry of National Defence and made no attempt to hide his separatist leanings. Chaput had been forbidden by his employer, the Minister of National Defence, from appearing at the symposium and espousing the separatist cause. When Chaput put in his appearance, the federal minister, Douglas Harkness, sent Chaput a telegram that arrived during the panel discussion. Its contents were read aloud. He was fired on the spot. Chaput did not flinch.

René Lévesque also attended the Congress. He was then Minister of National Resources in the Lesage government. When he spoke, he began by saying that he was "fed up" with all the talk about Canadian problems and that he was attending the symposium only because his boss, Mr. Lesage, had insisted that he do so.

I remember a remarkable, brilliant, and stormy debate that was conducted over a whole week, and André Laurendeau's reaction in *Le Devoir*. It was "an exciting experience," he wrote.

And now, twenty years later, what is left of that unusual Congress that had caught the attention of the whole country? Some of the participants have unfortunately passed on; some of the organizers have become Ministers; some Ministers have become Premiers; and Marcel Chaput is still absent from the payroll of the Department of National Defence.

The theme of our discussions was "The Canadian Experiment – Success or Failure." It would, no doubt, have been pretentious on our part to believe that the Congress would provoke changes in Confederation itself. Our hopes were much more modest. We were hoping – inexperienced students that we were – that our elders and our political leaders would use certain of the ideas and a major part of the enthusiasm generated by the Congress in evolving new approaches to old problems. But this did not seem to happen.

One of the consequences of the lack of response was that this group of young people, all of whom believed in a renewed Canadian federalism, are seriously asking themselves the same questions decades later. In debate on Quebec sovereignty, an important part of that group of friends was standing squarely on the "yes" side and another on the "no" side; and, unfortunately, in the intervening years, the attitudes have become more polarized, the ultimate question more brutal, and the stakes much bigger. And all this, because of a gesture or a series of gestures which no one dared to make.

Not long ago a friend in Quebec City told me how a group of young students were thinking of creating at Laval a kind of Estates-General representing all the different classes of the country – a National Congress whose objective would be to try, on another level surely, to definitely unlock the Canadian constitutional dossier. I mentally wished those students the best of luck, and a lot of patience.

We have been studied to death. Our self-analysis would make Freud look like a choir boy. We have developed our own peculiar cottage industry – highly paid and unproductive – in the field of constitutional reform.

Imagine what might have been accomplished in, say, the field of medical research if the same amount of time and energy, talent and money, had been available as in the field of federal-provincial relations. I became actively involved in the debate when I was nineteen. I am now forty-one and I can say with authority that I have played a peripheral role in erecting a monument to sterility. Others have been more prominent and eloquent in their waste of time than most of us. But we should find little satisfaction in this.

What seems to obsess many of our politicians are questions of exclusivity. They want more power for themselves and less for the other guy. The federal government, for example, says, "Give us the necessary authority to run the Post Office because it is a national enterprise." The provincial government says, "Give us exclusive authority over education because it is in provincial jurisdiction." There may be many compelling reasons why this should be done in both cases, but in some instances proven competence is not one of them.

The Canadian postal system has to be one of the worst in the civilized world. Its record is a litany of wildcat strikes, violence, interrupted service, and costly overruns. The postal deficit has increased in the last ten years from $67 million to $559 million. Despite a massive automation program, which the government implemented without consulting the postal unions, the total labour force has increased by 80 per cent from 36,000 ten years ago to 66,000 today.

On the other side of the street, elements of the educational system in the province of Quebec are an unrelieved disaster. In the last dozen years, the system of *Collèges d'Enseignement Général et Professionnel* (CEGEPs), when it is not strike-bound, has succeeded in turning out thousands of quasi-illiterates, many of whom cannot speak or write proper French or English and whose consequent inability to enter the work force in a productive manner is there for all to see. While this great educational bonanza was being generated, the government of Quebec had to announce that it could not account for $500 million in spending in the educational area. It is a comment on the extent to which Quebecers have become inured to government profligacy that this shocking revelation caused scarcely a murmur of protest.

Our politicians should know that these facts are not lost upon us. Obviously, some areas must indeed be reserved to the federal government. For example, the federal government must be empowered at all times to preserve the security and the integrity of the nation; to guarantee equality of services and opportunities; to ensure the enjoyment of our basic freedoms; and so on. Other fields clearly strike most of us as being clearly within the purview of a provincial authority.

But the dominant feature of our ongoing constitutional negotiations reflects not the foregoing but the philosophy of the late Samuel Gompers, one of America's first labour leaders. When asked what he wanted, he said: "More, more, always more." There is only so much to go around; there is only so much authority that can be diluted or transferred before the strength of a nation begins to ebb away.

Some people talk about Switzerland and Germany and every other kind of federalism known to man, pointing out their relative merits vis-à-vis the Canadian system. The Fathers of Confederation were not thinking of Switzerland when they began their discussions; they were thinking of Canada, a huge country with a tiny population, and they designed a political structure to preserve this unique and fragile identity on the northern half of a continent, dominated even then by the southern neighbour.

They were trying to devise a framework within which we could live and grow, a framework that was solid but flexible. They tried to create a society that would be decent and fair, where freedom would flourish, prosperity bloom—and most of all, a country whose virtues, attractions, and accomplishments would, of themselves, encourage national development and enhance the desire of people to remain Canadians because citizenship in the country was a privileged station in life; because, quite simply, it was good for them and good for their families. The Fathers of Confederation built better than they knew because in this entire world—and there are no exceptions – there is no nation with greater opportunities, greater tolerance, greater individual liberties, greater inbred traditions of justice and democracy than Canada. With all our failings – and we have many – our country stands out in bold relief as a place where freedom truly rings. For a nation of immigrants, we have not done too badly at all. Many say we have done well.

In any discussion of constitutional reform, I start from the premise of an indivisible Canada. The word is clear. It means exactly the same in English as it does in French. I do not believe in a theory of two nations, five nations, or ten nations. Surely we have learned that these "jeux de mots" merely obscure reality and inhibit effective dialogue. Nor do I believe in any concept that would give any one province an advantage over any other. Few would doubt, however, that there are real differences of outlook about the future shape of Canada because of varying perceptions of the proper role of a provincial government or a host of other valid reasons. Most of all, however, there is post-Referendum Quebec.

Quebec is different, very different. It is not strange or weird, it is just different. And the difference is rooted in language and culture. That is why the preservation and enhancement of these two instruments are so vital. That is why they must be protected and nurtured with a constancy and vigilance that can never be slackened. For English Canadians, comfortably ensconced in the protective linguistic cocoon that envelops all of North America, measures to ensure protection of the French language may sometimes seem silly and vexatious. But they are not. Such concerns are a deadly serious business.

Let me attempt to illustrate the difference between Quebec and the rest of the country. One of the best-known faces in Canada belongs to Knowlton Nash. In Mississauga, Ontario, or Swift Current, Saskatchewan, his presence causes a commotion. In Matane or St-Tite-des-Caps, Quebec, he could walk up and down the main street all day and not a soul would know he was there. The reason is that for French-speaking Canadians, Knowlton Nash does not exist – they have never heard of him in their lives. The Knowlton Nash for them is Bernard Derome, and he would be equally ignored in St. John's or Kelowna. But bring Bernard Derome to Matane and you would have people lining up for his autograph all day. It would probably astonish many Canadians to learn that for Quebecers, the national news is at 10:30 p.m., not at 10:00 p.m., and that the star of the show does not even wear glasses!

Language is the difference. This fundamental difference, exemplified in so many practical ways in day-to-day living, must be accommodated and recognized, together with other legitimate concerns of Canadians, in any constitutional revision or reform. The right to go to school, to pay a parking ticket, to argue with a civil servant, to buy a dozen eggs, to read a service manual at work – the right to do these things in one's language is at stake. There is no mystery; there is no conspiracy; there is only a fact of life.

During the Referendum debate, the federalist side made commitments to Quebecers. The message was clear: "Canada is a great country, more beneficial to Quebecers than would be René Lévesque's shining vision of a small independent nation-state. Vote 'No' on May 20 and we will make Canada even better. The symbols and the stuff of nationhood will be Canadianized. French Canadians will be made to feel even more at home throughout this splendid country of ours."

That was the message. Hundreds of us brought the message to every group in every area of Quebec. And on May 20, 1980, Quebecers voted for this case and for Canada. What has happened since then? What promises have we delivered on? What hope do we hold out for an early and amicable resolution of our constitutional problems? (You go to the head of the class if you answer all questions in the negative!)

2

If we examined carefully the positions taken on the subject of the Constitution by the leaders of the various political parties, we would find among them certain common points: the desire to patriate now; an amending formula that would not abuse Canadian customs; and the insertion of a charter of fundamental liberties. The equitable solution of this problem is a challenge of historic dimensions. The Resolution that was filed last month (October 1980) for study by Parliament was, according to some people, the best possible in the circumstances. After all, unanimity has never been an evident characteristic of the history of our country. And it seems to be even less so today.

The same solution was rejected by others because it was, in their judgement, imperfect, as it did not have the imprimatur of certain provincial authorities and because its effect would be to provoke a fundamental amendment to the Constitution by a foreign parliament. This was Quebec's position in this matter. Its historic rights must not be diminished in any constitutional adventure; I agree with this position.

And so, while governments quarrel, people wonder. Most Canadians have been labouring under the illusion that the Constitution was written for *them*. Most people I know view the BNA Act as a vital document, of somewhat obscure and uncertain origin, that was written to protect *them* and their families and neighbours – and set limits upon the power of the state to intrude upon their freedoms and the manner in which they live their lives. Very few of them could argue the merits of Section 91. All of them, however, can tell you what they think of Canada. In the Referendum, Quebecers were asked what they thought, and they responded with an overwhelming and affectionate reply to those entrusted with their temporary governance. I suspect you would get similar reactions if you asked the same question of other people in other provinces. We Canadians are a reasonably clever people. We can appreciate the magnificence of our own citizenship, if only because we witness daily what happens to others less privileged around the world. Even this great challenge cannot resist the application of such great Canadian qualities over the years as a spirit of generosity, a sense of tranquil courtesy, and the recognition that an honourable compromise is a sign of wisdom and not the admission of failure.

Important voices have been heard on this question. I suggest that the Resolution be referred to the Special Committee of the House, a Committee enlarged to include the Premiers of the provinces or their special delegates. If they wished, the Premiers could consult their legislatures prior to attendance, and the time-frames in the resolution could be adjusted to accommodate this. The debate would be entirely open to the public at all times.

61

There would be no sessions behind closed doors. Canadians could see and judge those who have been elected to serve them and determine if, in the interest of a more generous country, they have really answered an urgent and irresistible call to grandeur.

Litigation ultimately produces nothing but a winner and a loser along with an adversarial atmosphere. Debate among proud men and women, properly motivated and inspired, can produce a consensus, imperfect by definition but freely arrived at and hence more comfortably accepted and adhered to by those on whose behalf it was brought into being. So let us have this final constitutional forum in Ottawa in the hope that a favourable consensus will be referred back to the House for ultimate resolution.

By so doing the federal parliament will have gone the extra mile to ensure that, to the extent humanly possible, everyone was heard, all opinions were considered, all objections were entertained, and the honourable compromise found reasonable reflection in the final document.

This unusual procedure presents some obstacles itself. However, its saving grace is that it correctly localizes the problem and identifies the players – a Canadian problem will have been resolved by Canadians, here, in Canada. It would seem to me that these are the appropriate auspices under which a new basic Constitution should be brought into being.

The test of great leadership is to harmonize divergent views into an eloquent and thoughtful declaration of national purpose. I speak for many when I express the hope that on this sensitive and fundamental issue, Canada's political leadership will not be found wanting.

3

As we near the end of 1981, what should we think of the constitutional imbroglio? Should we have been surprised with the results?

Let us examine the situation with the calm of hindsight. Premier René Lévesque's mission in life is the independence of Quebec. This necessarily implies the dismemberment of Canada. Quebec would become, according to this hypothesis, a foreign country so far as the rest of Canada is concerned.

Mr. Lévesque is an honourable man. He was always honest about his political option. He stated it clearly. It is the number-one objective of the electoral program of his Parti Québécois. Moreover, Mr. Lévesque was most courageous when, in 1968, he left the security of the Liberal Party, thus endangering his whole political career, to give birth to his idea of independence. Rare are Canadian political figures who have taken such risks for their beliefs. This being said, why should we be surprised because Mr. Lévesque has refused to agree with a concrete gesture that would prove Canadian federalism is, in effect, flexible and can work? To do this would be to demolish all of his beliefs and vitiate his entire political action.

Has Quebec been isolated by its allies in Ottawa? Or rather, could it be that, by accepting Prime Minister Trudeau's referendum idea, Mr. Lévesque himself abandoned, without advance notice, his colleagues of the common front, who were all deeply opposed to such an idea? In fact, the form of the common front was deficient, and this in itself proved fatal. In the first place, its basis was most fragile and illusory – seven provinces favouring a renewed federalism and one in favour of a completely dismantled federalism. Was the euphoria in which the Quebec delegates found themselves united in a common front (thus permitting them to disguise their real intentions behind a smokescreen of "the Provinces") instrumental in bringing them to commit some of the most fundamental tactical errors? By trying to do indirectly and through third persons what the population of Quebec had formally forbidden them to do directly as a result of the Referendum in May 1980, did Quebec not follow a policy, the basis of which was flawed, and which could not withstand pressures of the most fundamental instincts of its associates? The ace of hearts had been played.

Must we be shocked by the abrupt disintegration of the common front before the following clear realities: a federal government determined to act quickly; a population – other Canadians as well as Quebecers – who, by a huge majority, wanted the constitutional guarantees enunciated; and allies whose vision of Canada was fundamentally different from that of a separatist government?

In an editorial in *Le Devoir*, Michel Roy wrote: "In an electoral joust or a leadership convention, these duels of tactics and these fights of shadows in the night present an interest which captivates and even amuses. But when they concern the future of a rather shaken country, the mishaps and intrigues of hallways only delight thoughtless persons." In a modest way, I have known the harsh realities represented by "certain nights in Ottawa" of which Mr. Roy speaks. For this reason, I understand and sympathize with the disappointment felt by Mr. Lévesque. It was a brief affair, abruptly terminated. But politics are for big boys. If one is incapable of accepting the after-effects without unseemly bitterness, one should stay home.

I have the impression that the brilliance of the tactics of a Marcel Pépin or the engaging personality of a Louis Laberge, which hides the talent of a first-rate negotiator, might have better served Quebec than an army of theologically minded civil servants of the PQ who, it would appear, have not yet learned that the human and acceptable answers to complex questions are not always found in the tranquility of our best universities.

Did anyone steal Quebec's historic veto in constitutional matters, or did Quebec not cede it when the Supreme Court decided, following a request from Quebec itself, that unanimity was no longer required? And did Quebec not sign a document ceding its traditional veto in favour of the Victoria Amending Formula? At that point it had lost the ace of clubs.

Has anyone imposed on Quebec linguistic limitations, or did it not exchange this power in 1977 in a proposal put to the provincial Premiers at St. Andrew's? "Protect the linguistic rights of minorities outside Quebec, and we will guarantee the rights of minorities here." That is exactly what the Ottawa agreement has accomplished. It is therefore the ace of diamonds that was played.

The government of Quebec has but one card left – that of bilateral negotiation. One solution is offered immediately to the parties as a first step to the resolution of the three main points at issue: the Ryan Formula. If Claude Ryan had the courage to risk the disintegration of his own caucus in order to promote the superior interests of Quebec, we must now, as Quebecers, honour him by accepting as valuable the draft solutions he has submitted concerning the points at issue.

Like many others, I have always believed that constitutional reform would, in some way, reinforce the position of Quebec and that of the other provinces, if they so wished. Because of evident cultural and linguistic reasons, Quebec will always need a protective device to ensure the survival of the only French-speaking people in North America.

The federal government, through a remodelling of the Constitution, has obtained the enshrining of the rights of linguistic minorities outside Quebec, and I can only rejoice in this. However, such a noble and valuable accomplishment should not be tarnished by the possible reduction of Quebec's powers to legislate in the fields which are particularly crucial to this province.

I recognize that the day after a brutal and somewhat difficult confrontation, people get exercised and words sometimes go beyond thoughts. Mr. Lévesque's bitterness was displayed in full daylight and his gratuitous and petty warning to the English minority in Quebec neither impressed me nor honoured him, particularly as Quebec had always treated its minorities with justice. If the government of Quebec broke with this tradition, it would only be at its own risk. The verdict of historians, including French-Canadian historians, would be extremely harsh.

But if Mr. Trudeau feels victorious, he should remember the words of Churchill, who, God knows, knew defeat and disappointment and finally the most exalting moments: "In victory, magnanimity."

One should not forget that Messrs. Lévesque and Trudeau were elected to be our servants and not our masters. They are there to execute the population's will, the will of the people. Therefore, they had a heavy and joint moral obligation to meet alone – without any advisers or technocrats – as soon as possible, in order to come to an honourable agreement which would permit us to take action in the priority areas of social and economic development.

In other words, Messrs. Trudeau and Lévesque must now put aside any sense of partisanship, any electoral consideration, any idea of provincial or federal victory, and work together toward a clearly superior and more noble goal: that of the welfare of the ordinary citizen.

To this end, and if it is not unduly presumptuous on my part, I would like to put at their disposal for their deliberations, our guest house at Schefferville. They could not possibly find a more serene place, a more propitious climate or a warmer welcome. It is a place they like and where they are liked. These two great leaders from Quebec have received from the population of Schefferville a vote of confidence of astonishing proportions at the last elections. This would be a magnificent occasion for them to re-attune themselves with the daily reality, away from the hallways of large metropolitan hotels, to find solutions for the people, close to the people.

This meeting is urgent because if Quebec is not in it, what is to become of the famous "Canadian duality"? Should the word be simply stricken from our vocabulary? What would be done about the deplorable lot reserved for women and native people, for example? Should we now pretend that their fundamental rights as human beings are of secondary importance and will be settled maybe, some day, when we have the time?

Our two leaders will find, right there in Schefferville, some 500 feet away from the house, extremely legitimate representatives of these two groups, should they require living and real advisers in these fields.

I, for one, have learned that nothing is cast in concrete! I am very happy about the remarkable progress made in the constitutional dossier but I will not feel less virile or more traumatized if the whole process is not finished by Christmas. I have nothing against Easter and I have always loved spring.

Let us now take time to complete the dossier with honour. Those who will refuse to negotiate in good faith in such circumstances and in the face of such high stakes, ultimately will have to pay the price on the occasion of the next election or referendum.

I am a Canadian and a Quebecer, proud of my country and my province. I say this simply, without embarrassment, without hesitation, and without ambiguity.

Félix-Antoine Savard one day wrote: "*Heureux les hommes et les peuples raccordés.*" Happy are men and people when united. That is my hope for all and my most profound desire for our country.

66

Chapter VIII
The Essence of Federalism

1

What about the future? Let us think about the year 2000. Believe it or not, we are much closer to it than to the year 1960, which marked the beginning of the great upheavals of the Quiet Revolution.

What does Quebec's North Shore have to offer to future, job-creating investors?

1. Natural resources unparalleled in Quebec.
2. A highly specialized and reliable work force.
3. A population whose basic values reflect the best dimensions of a human and accessible conservatism.
4. A trade unionism which, after some difficult moments, is becoming more mature, rejects excessive solutions, and accepts its role as a vital partner in economic development.
5. Professionals in the medical, legal, and engineering fields who supply a service that easily rivals equivalent services provided in large metropolitan centres.
6. A social and cultural infrastructure capable of fulfilling the needs of a growing and demanding population.
7. Municipalities governed by individuals who have a real knowledge of the real problems of an investor and who treat the latter as a friend and not as an enemy.
8. A service industry capable of creating jobs and of meeting the needs of large business.
9. An abundance of that vital resource, hydroelectricity, right under our noses.
10. A highway system and, particularly, a marine transportation and port system that will, as years go by, become the

envy of competitors elsewhere in the world.

I foresee during this period a degree of development and prosperity without precedent in our history. If we look at the basic industries here – pulp and paper, aluminum, grain trans-shipment, etc. – we soon realize that there will be a substantial expansion in each of these sectors. In the case of the Iron Ore Company, for example, it is true that we are going through a difficult period because of the international market for steel, which has been greatly affected by a decline in the world economy, but we are not a dying company. On the contrary, we still have over 6,000 employees, a total payroll of $200 million a year, and payments for materials and services, equipment, taxes, royalties, and interest in the order of $515 million. We therefore generate business in the neighbourhood of $750 million a year. There is no doubt that the market will strengthen eventually and that we will play a growing role in the regional economy of the North Shore and Labrador.

It seems to me that the situation will be similar for the other principal industries on the North Shore. The expansion planned for Reynolds at Baie Comeau reflects the requirements of the international aluminum market this region can fulfil because of its manpower, the availability of electricity, and its harbour facilities. Another reason for being optimistic is the possibility of the development of our hydroelectric resources in Quebec, let us hope, in co-operation with Newfoundland, notwithstanding the rather tense relations between the neighbouring provinces since the events at the Constitutional Conference in Ottawa. The present contract between Quebec and Newfoundland for electric power from Churchill Falls does not reflect in any way the new economic and energy realities that have developed since the OPEC crisis. The contract cannot remain unchanged for its duration, that is, until the year 2041. It would be like asking Newfoundland to sell to Quebec fifty-five million barrels of oil a year at $1.80 a barrel when the same barrel sells for $35 elsewhere today. The contract then requires that Newfoundland sell us, during the last twenty-five years of the life of the contract, the equivalent of fifty-five million barrels of oil a year at the splendid price of $1.20 a barrel. And what price do you think you would be paying at that time on the world market for a barrel of oil?

I recognize that there exists a duly signed contract that covers this complex question. I will concede that the contract is strictly legal. But, as was recently stated by the Supreme Court in connection with the Constitution, a document may be "strictly legal" and at the same time be completely deficient in the areas of "convention" and "equity." The inequality and absence of fair play in the contract in question is obvious. Simple decency and the most elementary spirit of justice demand its immediate renegotiation.

If there is a segment of the Canadian population which has, in the past, experienced unfavourable legal and contractual situations, it is that of Quebec. Because we have experienced such situations and have understood the effects of their injustice, we certainly do not wish their presence in other parts of the population. We have a right to our visions as well as to our great dreams. The amicable settlement of the conflict would have dramatic consequences. It would unfreeze huge amounts of money and would bring about a historic development in Labrador and New Quebec.

Apart from the development of the sites along the Lower Churchill, which would supply the equivalent of twenty-six million barrels of oil a year, at a cost of over $7 billion, there are five other rivers whose headwaters are in Labrador and power sites are in Quebec. Such a situation therefore requires the joint participation of the provinces in their development. They, alone, can supply 3,000 megawatts or the equivalent of thirty-five million more barrels of oil a year.

A global program for the development of these possibilities would imply a construction program of $20 billion over a period of fifteen years and would provide many thousands of well-paid jobs. The effects on the North Shore would be immediate and dramatic. Everything that accompanies such a large development – roads, railways, mining exploration, service industries, professional services, the creation of new northern cities – is to be envisaged.

The biggest service the appropriate provincial governments could render to the citizens of this vast region would be to settle this problem in an equitable manner with the least possible delay. The settlement would, in itself, give rise to a new economic impetus that would bring a wave of astonishing benefits to the whole region.

2

Negativism and criticism are commodities of diminishing attractiveness to a beleaguered nation. Critical times require examples of vision and courage, not articulation of pessimism and despair. Canadians want to hear fresh ideas and creative thinking. They are fed up to the teeth with carping and fault-finding. They want concrete illustrations of co-operation among management, labour, government, and political parties of all stripes. They want to hear, from us and from others, specific solutions to immediate problems and not vague, airy-fairy theories about what we will do, if, when, some day, somehow.

Let us not be afraid of the Grits stealing our thunder. If we have ideas for a new beginning and a new direction for this country – and we have – let us spell them out one by one, item by item, issue by issue, now, when the people of Canada need hope. Let us give them that hope and that confidence to know that a new era and a new prosperity will dawn with a new government that knows exactly where it is going and precisely what it is going to do when it gets there.

3

This is quite simply the most blessed nation on the face of this earth. There is nothing that Canadians cannot do in a reasonable and thoughtful way once they set their minds to it. We must begin by purging the negativism and the vitriol from our public life and our private manner.

It is not an indictable offence for a union leader like Dennis McDermot to utter a civil word about Immigration Minister Lloyd Axworthy's work-sharing program. It does not diminish Pierre Trudeau's virility to acknowledge that Newfoundland's position on the offshore issue may indeed be worth a second look. And it is not a crippling indignity for the government of Quebec to deal sensibly with Ottawa on all matters of importance to Quebecers, with neither slogans nor suspicions accompanying each move.

We must begin again to understand that our success – or occa-

70

sional lack of it – is merely a reflection of our capacity as a people to meet challenge and change. We must recognize in a civilized way that, as Canadians, we are dedicated to a common goal, namely, the well-being of our citizens and a contribution to those less favoured elsewhere in the world. All of this is inhibited by constant confrontation, personal or political, which poisons atmospheres and makes progress impossible. It leaves lots of room for vigorous, partisan debate.

We must throw off this black mood of pessimism and despair that grips our national consciousness and reflect upon the greatness we have achieved and the opportunities to come. Let us not blame any one group, including governments, for our problems, although it is tempting to do so. The incompetence of the present federal government has been elevated to a rare art form. In spite of such governments, this nation has attained heights of accomplishment, a quality of life, a standard of justice, a sense of fair play, a respect for the dignity of man, a feeling of compassion for the underprivileged, all of which are envied by most nations in the world.

What was accomplished here by ordinary Canadians assuming responsibility, through generations of sacrifice and commitment, in an atmosphere of tolerance and mutual respect, is clear for all to see. Let us recapture that spirit, that belief in ourselves, that appreciation of what a strongly united Canada can be for us and our children and, together, let us move on with the job of building a world-class nation that will honour its citizens and be of service to the world.

Chapter IX
Leadership Today

1

Today the Quebec construction industry, now the $10-billion-a-year economic motor of the province of Quebec, is essentially free from violence. It has been without serious labour difficulties since May 1, 1975. It was not always so.

The government of Quebec appointed the Cliche Royal Commission in April 1974. Along with Robert Cliche (chairman) and Guy Chevrette, I was a member. The three of us, as Royal Commissioners charged with an important responsibility in Quebec, became close allies, intimate collaborators, and fast friends.

We formed an unlikely trio on the Quebec stage. Robert Cliche was a Liberal who became Leader of the NDP in Quebec and an outstanding Chief Justice and Royal Commissioner; Guy Chevrette, a logger's son from Joliette who became a teacher, vice-president of the Quebec Teachers' Union, and today a cabinet minister in the Parti Québécois government; and I, a Conservative lawyer, son of a unionized electrician from Baie Comeau. We joined in an unforgettable challenge: to clean up a vital sector of the economy that was corrupt from top to bottom. The tentacles of the corruption reached into surprising areas of Quebec's economic and political structures. If the task at hand was daunting, the consequences of failure would have been ominous. Such rot, if not excised, could spread to all other areas of economic endeavour and undermine the very basis of a democratic society, namely the rule of law itself.

We met for 364 days, held hearings, and presented our report with its 132 recommendations ready to be enacted into law. The costs of the commission to the taxpayer were the lowest on record. The unprecedented violence that had plagued the Quebec construction industry and its workers for a decade had come to an end.

I shall never forget those challenging and tumultuous days. Our inspiration was the sense that we were helping to free thousands of ordinary workers—honest, decent, hard-working people—from the madness that had overtaken an entire industry. Overwhelming public support was our encouragement. Respect for the rule of law was our objective. Peace on construction sites throughout Quebec was our reward.

Then Guy Chevrette and I, along with many others, experienced a day of overwhelming sadness. Robert Cliche, a man of clear brilliance, uncommon warmth, delightful humour, infectious charm, and genuine leadership was buried in September, 1978, in his beloved hometown of St-Joseph-de-Beauce. He was fifty-eight. His contribution to Quebec and Canada was impressive. His enrichment of the lives of his friends was immeasurable.

2

On March 21, 1974, a man named Yvon Duhamel boarded a D-8 bulldozer and drove it wilfully and unerringly into the electric generators at James Bay. Within moments, he had secured for himself an inglorious footnote in history. His deliberate and criminal action resulted in the evacuation of the largest construction job site in the history of Quebec, the paralysis of Premier Robert Bourassa's $15-billion "Project of the Century," and direct costs to the consumers of Quebec of $35 million. For his criminal action, Mr. Duhamel got ten years in a federal penitentiary.

This was symptomatic of a decade of excess everywhere. American politicians were in constant danger of being shot in the streets. Business executives were kidnapped and held to ransom. Fratricidal wars were waged in the name of religion. Canada was not immune. In October 1970, a diplomat was abducted and a cabinet minister slain, to mention but the most tragic of our collective misfortunes.

In the mid-sixties, the Quiet Revolution had paused for breath. There was no relationship of cause and effect, but by that time certain things had become unfashionable. It was unfashionable, for example, to proclaim any belief in the federal concept of government; it was unfashionable to acknowledge any possible benefits from our free-enterprise system because no venture was considered of value unless big government was involved; it was unfashionable to stand firm on any moral issue because, in the minds of many, anti-clericalism and its attendant social postures were the wave of the future; and, most of all, it was unfashionable to contemplate anything but a totally unionized society because, we were told, politicized trade unionism was to be the collective salvation.

I remember well the alacrity with which part of the Quebec media responded to these challenges. Each night brought Louis Laberge or Marcel Pépin or Yvon Charbonneau in living colour on the "National News" with their three-minute homilies. These invariably involved vitriolic denunciations of elected governments, business, social standards, each other, and anything else that happened to be lying around that day. There have been few recorded cases in Canada involving such remarkable – and misplaced – glorification of individuals.

My father was active in his union throughout his working life. I believe strongly in the value of vigorous trade unionism. Unions are indispensable instruments of social progress. The benefits of collective action are there for all to see. But trade unions and management associations are precisely what they are called. Political parties and elected governments are quite another thing.

If we live in a democratic country, all of us must accept the majesty – and the weaknesses – of the concept. There can be no compromise where the supremacy of Parliament is involved. In Quebec, as elsewhere, we try to follow the basic rules of the game. During the mid-sixties, however, thoughtful observers began asking whether the duly elected government or highly vocal pressure groups were exercising real and effective power. In the United Kingdom, the question was straightforward: can the government enact legislation without the prior approval of the Trades Union Congress? And the answer seemed to be in the negative. Little wonder that, having passively accepted such a degree of erosion of the supremacy of Parliament, the British government today should be so hard pressed to explain its own inadequacies.

But we were not to be outdone by the British. On March 24,

1971, a parliamentary commission of the Quebec National Assembly was in the process of analysing a piece of legislation. Led by André Desjardins, the director of the Quebec Federation of Labour's construction wing, thirty strong-armed men invaded the National Assembly, disrupted proceedings, intimidated members, assaulted other trade unionists, damaged four automobiles, left Quebec City, and laughed all the way home. No charges were ever laid, even though the witnesses – indeed, the victims – were our duly elected Members of the National Assembly, to say nothing of the institution itself.

Little wonder, then, that Yvon Duhamel decided to destroy the James Bay Project. He never expected to be penalized for his actions – after all, if one can assault the Quebec National Assembly with impunity, what is wrong with a little friendly violence on a construction site? Such was the legacy of a decade of permissiveness, governmental inaction, and neglect in Quebec, particularly in the construction industry.

In large part, this was the reason for the creation of the Cliche Royal Commission, sworn in on May 3, 1974. Generally speaking, its mandate was to analyse the conduct of all those associated directly or indirectly with the construction industry to ensure that in the future basic union freedoms would be maintained. This was not an unchallenging task, inasmuch as the construction industry is, by far, the single most important industry in Quebec. The $6 billion expended annually in this field (in 1975), the 150,000 people it employs, the multiplier effect it has on all sectors of economic growth testify eloquently to its importance.

The Commission held public hearings for eighty days, during which time 279 witnesses were heard from all walks of life. During the course of these hearings, almost a thousand exhibits were filed and analysed by the Commission. It was as a result of the evidence adduced in public that the existence of an organized system of corruption became apparent. This system, which had the effect of seriously diminishing individual freedom in trade unions, was certainly not easy to unearth or define for a number of reasons, chief among these being the fact that the main protagonists were, when called upon to testify, suddenly afflicted with very severe cases of selective amnesia. In some instances, this contagious illness causes deafness – witnesses who could not recall previously corroborated testimony; in other cases, it induced blindness – witnesses who could not see acts of violence and criminality committed before their very eyes.

But anyone who had eyes to see and ears to hear knows full well that the system of unfettered corruption and violence that existed in the construction industry in Quebec was entirely without parallel in the history of labour relations in Canada. Other jurisdictions, such as Ontario, made strenuous efforts to lay claim to this dubious honour, but the Commissioners felt that, on the merits of the case, the award really should go to Quebec.

Some time ago, the Justice Department, concerned about the rising wave of violence in the construction industry, initiated a series of police operations to ascertain precisely what was going on and what could be done about it. In the course of this initiative, known as "Operation Raymond," a substantial number of telephone conversations were wiretapped by the appropriate police officers working within the framework of the law. Records of these conversations and all the information accumulated by the various police forces were made available to us. It must be said that, at the outset, we were reluctant to use these telephone conversations because of our concern about the civil liberties of people who might be called to testify before us. Faced, however, with a growing mountain of mendacity and a series of witnesses whose proclivity for deceit was no less monumental, the Commission had no choice but to confront the perjurers with the clear evidence of their crimes.

Clearly, the most spectacular revelation of our hearings related to the foregoing. It became obvious, as we dug deeper, that a relatively small group of men had succeeded, at least in part, in erecting a new set of social standards in Quebec. The hallmarks of this new era were lawlessness and violence. Illegality was the key to success. Monopoly of strategic services and industries was to be the end result. In quest of this domination, the laws that apply to all were breached regularly, enthusiastically, and with impunity. The word "anarchy" is not too strong a term to describe accurately the Quebec construction industry during those years.

No industry is so important and no group of men is so powerful as to be permitted to impose its own base and scurrilous set of standards upon an entire province. Any such attempt, from whatever quarter, must be resisted with every energy because our collective, social, and moral standards, with all their imperfections, are those by which we live our lives and by which we consent to be governed. That is why the Commission set out in blunt and uncompromising language its assessment of a brutal—indeed, a criminal—system and of those people responsible for its existence. We believed then, and we believe now, that this assault on the basic values of our society must be repulsed, and its legacy excised, lest it spread to other fields of endeavour.

How did so much corruption come about? Sometime in the future an appropriate explanation will be given by some thoughtful historian. In the meantime, here are three reasons for the corruption. The causes were: (1) politicization of trade unions; (2) management complicity; (3) non-enforcement of the law.

In the early 1960s, when asked about his government's attitude regarding collective bargaining in the public service, Premier Jean Lesage replied: "*La Reine ne négocie pas avec ses sujets.*" The Queen does not negotiate with her subjects. How delightfully quaint that statement sounds now. Not only does the Queen negotiate with her subjects today, she often is required to do so in an atmosphere of hostility and rancour that could make even the most bitter political opponents in Canada look like a bunch of choir boys.

In 1971, Bill 46 set out the bargaining structure in the health and education sectors, and provided for government participation on the management team as well as for province-wide bargaining in these areas. By insisting upon a general salary policy for the entire public sector and a common bargaining posture regarding hospitals and schools, the government, unwittingly, I suspect, forced the unions into a common front for collective-bargaining purposes. This new grouping, representing some 250,000 people, shortly became a political instrument of unquestioned strength. Because they were on opposite sides of the table on bread-and-butter matters, they quickly took opposite sides of the fence on political issues. The government soon found itself with an official opposition, in everything except elected status.

The bitterness quickly accelerated. Defiance of a court injunction in 1972 sent Messrs. Laberge, Pépin, and Charbonneau to jail. The *La Presse* strike was used as a symbol of worker oppression. The unions threw themselves into an aggressive campaign against the government in the 1973 election. Positions and people became irreconcilable.

In this two-way fight, there were two quasi-winners: the government and the union establishment. There were two sure losers, the public and the worker – the forgotten guy who pays his dues, pays his taxes, respects the law, and does an honest day's work. He became the tragedy of politicization. His interests were subordinated to the political aspirations of the leadership. Equally tragic is the fact that when his leaders now present legitimate demands on his behalf, they are perceived by the government as self-serving incursions of political adversaries and are dealt with as such.

Good laws are of little value unless they are enforced. Nonenforcement is an insidious thing because it breeds a gentle but progressive suspicion in the minds of the governed that a statute need not apply to all, that exceptions can be made, that demonstrations can supplant debate, that Parliament is in fact somewhat less than supreme.

This is not to say that, in drafting legislation, government should ignore the voice of reason from any quarter. Only an exceptionally foolish and vain group of men and women would do that. But when our duly elected parliaments have spoken, be it in Ottawa, Queen's Park, or Quebec City, there can be no turning back, no exceptions, and, in the face of resistance, no compromise.

I realize that politics is still the art of the possible, that our society is highly complex, and that running a government is not an easy thing. But in regard to Parliament itself, its Members are merely custodians of its supremacy. Anything that diminishes its magnificence, impairs its effectiveness, or erodes its authority is a grievous act.

As Commissioners, we were dismayed to hear a Minister of the Crown, in sworn testimony before us, say that he was "powerless" to enforce legislation. And we were shocked to hear a Deputy Minister say: "When the unions have a gun to your head, what do you do? You cave in."

And cave in they did on a regular, ongoing basis. Small wonder that growing numbers of citizens began to decide for themselves what laws they would obey and what laws they would not. Unless this trend is firmly arrested, one day we, as Canadians, shall all pay a heavy price for our indifference.

In the federal sector alone, since public-service bargaining began, there have been innumerable unlawful work stoppages. A vital question in Canada today is what has happened to blur the distinction in workers' minds between "legal" and "illegal" strikes? What causes a Postal Union leader to say, "To hell with the public"? What causes longshoremen to hold a meeting to decide if they will obey federal legislation and then decide they will defy the legislation?

The answer is neither "in our stars" nor in "the universe unfolding as it should." The answer is in our leadership.

Leadership—that is the question today. If we are led by people who accept sacrifice themselves before inflicting hardship on others; who practise the virtues of thrift, compassion, and humility before exacting them from us; who respect Parliament and its institutions before castigating those who have walked the slippery road of defiance; who tell us the truth even when they think we do not want to hear it—if we have that kind of leadership, and have it we must, Canada may yet fulfil that most splendid promise of her youth.

Chapter X
A View from Baie Comeau

1

I always find myself at home in Baie Comeau, surrounded by people from all parts of the North Shore. Here one may find a sense of regional solidarity, a spirit of mutual aid which has been instrumental in building this corner of our country. This instinct for co-operation has always enabled us to understand one another, to back each other up. Evidence of its presence may be found at each moment in our short history. It is all the more important today because it assists us in supporting those among us who, through a quirk of nature or by accident, find themselves less than well-equipped to face the necessities of everyday life. I would not recognize the North Shore if I could not find groups and associations here whose vocation it is to enhance the quality of life. They extend from Schefferville to Sacré-Coeur. This means that those among us who suffer from a physical or a mental handicap may count on all the other citizens of the North Shore. That is the way we were brought up here.

2

I have so many memories of growing up in Baie Comeau that I hardly know where to begin. I remember, for instance, our family's annual, 300-mile trip to Quebec City in my father's old 1938 Pontiac. My father at that time was inclined to think of himself as a Gilles Villeneuve. He would begin our fourteen-hour odyssey at four in the morning – my parents, the six children, the dog, fourteen sandwiches, and a six-pack – to begin a mad race over unpaved roads to catch the ferry at Bersimis, followed by an heroic gallop to catch the ferry at Baie Ste-Catherine, followed by a leisurely ride at seventy miles an hour to Quebec; the children crying, the dog barking, my father grinding his teeth, and my mother saying the beads for the third time that day!

Many remember an imposing billboard situated at the entrance to the village of Sacré-Coeur. On this billboard appeared a coloured picture of the Lord with the caption: "Why do you use the name of the Lord in vain?" During my entire childhood, I always thought that the message was directed exclusively at my father!

I have fond memories, too, of the parties at Alfred Arsenault's on Laurier Street on New Year's Eve – a *réveillon* which, for Blair Touchie, once lasted for three days. I remember the arrival here in 1955 of a whole colony of Scots at the start of the construction of Canadian British Aluminum Company, and the utter amazement of the *habitués* of Taverne aux Amis when we learned that the men wore skirts and rode bicycles. For those of us who like me were dreaming of the Chrysler of the year, just like the one owned by Jean-Baptiste Kirouac, this was a great disappointment!

I remember the endless and unforgiving winters, isolated as we were, without regular newspapers, without television, with few modern means of communication, except perhaps the voice of Jean Brisson of CJBR in Rimouski which was, in some ways, our link with the outside world.

I cherish my memories, imperishable memories of a father who, during his entire life, held down two jobs to provide for the needs of his family with neither complaint nor regret; memories also of the tenderness of a mother whose constant thought was for her family and the happiness of her home; memories of our neighbours and friends who shared the same values and whose sacrifice and devotion gave birth to this marvel which is the North Shore.

We had a happy community and family life. It was a pleasant place to live. We felt safe, completely sheltered from the events which were beginning to perturb Quebec society elsewhere.

3

The first people to venture into this remote area, with a few exceptions, were not civil servants; the first people were you and your parents; and men like Monseigneurs Labrie and Bélanger, Drs. Binet and Thurber, Arthur Schmon, Napoleon A. Comeau, and George Humphrey. Baie Comeau and Sept-Iles were not built with government funds. Governments do not have money. They use our money, yours and mine.

Nothing is more offensive to me than to hear a civil servant, sitting comfortably in a luxurious office in Quebec or in Ottawa, speak of "government money" or "government subsidies." Apart from the federal government's capacity to print dollars and that of the provincial governments to borrow – which they do at a ridiculous rate – all the money, all the wealth in Canada comes from the taxpayers' pockets, be they individuals or corporations, and from no one else. The creators of jobs, management, and workers – the productive element of our society – are the ones who provide our government leaders with the elegant lives they now enjoy.

Because of the increasing amounts required by the various levels, governments appear to believe that they are better equipped to spend our money than we are. This is a philosophy of state-directed planning which is profoundly paternalistic and inherently erroneous and which, in my opinion, will be rebuffed here as it has been elsewhere and in the very near future. The disappointment of the great middle class in Canada is now at its peak. It will be followed by despair, as summer follows spring.

Therefore, the great risks involved in the development of the North Shore were taken by investors – some of whom were foreigners, it is true – and by us – the workers, foremen, and management. And we have all, as it should be, been rewarded for our efforts.

Was it a demeaning life experience – as some fancy-pants leftists would lead us to believe, those who now discourage new capital from entering Canada and penalize the existing pool – for you, for me, for many others who found here a sense of belonging; an important degree of tolerance and pride; moral strength; a legitimate ambition to do, to build, to acquire and to share; the capacity to suffer defeat, sometimes with difficulty, and to start again toward new challenges?

These are qualities which were instilled into us, perhaps unknowingly, by an independent and audacious life on the North Shore. Such are the values and liberties we have acquired here and which are slowly being taken away from us, quietly, gradually, surreptitiously, by our leaders behind a smokescreen called "democratic collectivism." For me, it is just like an insidious illness which will, inescapably, diminish our strength and our duties as independent citizens.

If governments were so intelligent, if they were such good administrators, so skilful – and I say this without any partisan spirit – how could the following facts be explained?

- A rate of inflation of 13 per cent a year.
- A rate of unemployment close to 10 per cent.
- A rate of interest over 20 per cent.
- A $500-million gap in the Quebec education budget which went unnoticed for many years.
- A deficit of $5 billion in Quebec.
- A deficit of $13 billion in Ottawa.

And so on. To show how far removed certain of our leaders are from the real problems, consider the following:

- A guy from Baie Comeau who earns $500 a week and spends $600 has a problem. A government that does the same thing does not have a care in the world.
- An employer in Hauterive who disagrees on an important question with his striking employees has a problem. Not so at the government level.
- Individuals in Sept-Iles who would call their neighbours in Port-Cartier "vassals," "traitors," "public liars," or "sell-outs," and do this every day, would have a problem; not so at the government level. It is simply current practice. (This is the background and the political climate in which constitutional and economic negotiations are conducted in Canada.)

The spirit of generosity, the respect for a neighbour's dignity, the acknowledgement of a job well done, the acceptance of an honourable compromise as being a step forward, the courage of admitting that you are not always right and that your neighbour is not always wrong – all these magnificent qualities have charac-

terized those who have built and civilized this extraordinary terri-
tory which is the North Shore; and all these qualities are being
replaced at certain levels by an institutionalized cynicism and
negativism which is spread about by some of our public leaders in
a progressively alarming, off-hand manner.

Chapter XI
Service to Others

1

What can one tell a graduating class in the 1980s? Probably very little it does not already know. When I graduated from college, Grattan O'Leary, the famed journalist, told us that "a good education does not provide you with a standard of living. It provides you with a standard of life." That was true. When I graduated from law school, another distinguished Canadian told us that "there are no great men—there are only ordinary men who rise to meet great challenges." That turned out to be true as well.

This suggests one thing we may not realize until tomorrow—gone forever will be the supportive parents, the understanding teachers, the summer jobs, and the delights that attach to an unencumbered existence. Oh, they will always be around; but the coldness that sometimes envelops reality comes from the daily recognition that responsibility is no longer a word to be spelled but a commitment to be honoured. And it must be honoured every day to family, employer, associates, and community.

But with progressive responsibility reasonably assumed comes opportunity. When I was a kid in Baie Comeau, I listened to a CBC radio program called "Opportunity Knocks" with John Adaskin. I wondered then about the mystery of the golden stories behind the celebrated voices and the good things that had happened to them in places far away. And I sometimes wondered what it might be like. My fertile imagination had played tricks on me because I find there is little mystery in some of those matters today.

My experience is not untypical and my observations I imagine could be repeated by many others in many walks of life across this country. Simply put, they are that we are a people many times blessed. The opportunities that exist for all of us to live challenging and bountiful lives are equalled only by the magnificence of the country that provides them. There is nothing wrong with a little luck or good fortune. But no substitute has, to my knowledge, yet been invented for hard work and innovative commitment.

We live in a world dominated by one factor – change. It is the one constant that will set our pace, create our problems, accommodate our talents, and define our frontiers. The world in twenty years will bear slim resemblance to what we see around us today.

But certain things do not change. They are, in my judgement, the attractive anachronisms which will bear as much relevance at any given time in the future as they have provided valued guidance in the past. Among other things, they are a sense of tolerance, an appreciation of friendship, a pride of family, and a desire to acquit one's tasks honourably and well.

Many years ago, John Morley wrote that "the mind is not a vessel to be filled; it is a hearth to be lighted." A man may be a great scientist, technician, or doctor and yet not be educated. The reason is that education, true education, is something that concerns the understanding heart, that concerns the spirit, that concerns the human soul.

If you can live your life in a reasonable manner, guided by these or similar benchmarks, you will spend little time in search of illusory or ephemeral goals, however enchanting they might appear at first blush. You will have lived a full and rich life which will have found expression in an enhancement of your own attributes combined with service to others. There will be no compulsion to search out uncommon standards of success – though these may come in a natural way – because you will have lived by your own.

It is said that "young men have visions and old men dream dreams." Take a good look around. Some of your classmates may have the vision to cure an illness, to create an empire, to heal a child. They will have enhanced their God-given gifts with sacrifice and hard work. For others, accomplishments may be less glamorous but no less noble. When asked by passersby why she was piling rock upon rock in an empty field, a young girl replied simply: "I am building a cathedral."

There is no uniformity of architecture or requirement for grandeur in such an endeavour. It is an entirely subjective process. Indeed, some of our most lasting and endearing institutions are marked by a degree of simplicity and a measure of inner strength. And so it is in the manner in which we live our lives. You must retain both a sense of humility and a sense of humour. When asked for his comments after he had lost the 1952 presidential election, Adlai Stevenson replied: "I'm like the boy who stubbed his toe – it hurts too much to laugh and I'm too old to cry." These virtues, which all of us have in varying degrees, are to be cherished and nurtured because they alone will supply perspective in moments of exultation and strength in periods of dismay.

Following the tragedy of the Bay of Pigs, President John F. Kennedy observed that "victory has one hundred fathers and defeat is an orphan." Moments of trial and failure are important events in human lives because we shall be judged by the manner in which we respond to them. Sadness is not a commodity that guards itself jealously. It spreads itself around with a liberality and a lack of discrimination that startles and shocks. Only the most favoured may ultimately state that sadness has rarely intruded upon their lives. Most of us come to know it in a real and heartbreaking way.

But the joys of living life fully, the pleasures of accomplishment, the pride of service to others ultimately combine to prevail, to produce equilibrium and continuity in our daily conduct. Keep alive the thought that laughter is a beautiful thing. Scholars have noted that Shakespeare makes the jesters practically the only really sensible people in his plays. Malcolm Muggeridge certainly knows a little about laughter and about life. He once said: "What is most needed both in order to go on laughing and in order to understand what life is truly about is the virtue of humility; to be able to know, to observe and recognize the great disparity between human performance and human aspiration, which really is the essence of our human existence."

One has only to reflect on the history and culture of Newfoundland and its prospects to appreciate the opportunities for service that await one. There is an industrial base here that one day will be the envy of many – hydro power, oil and gas, fisheries, mining, pulp and paper, tourism – it is all here.

There will be remarkable growth in Newfoundland but such growth often brings difficult problems. There are traditions to be honoured here and a lifestyle to be preserved. There is a vigorous outport feeling of self-reliance to be respected and a Labradorian sense of isolation to be harmonized with the provincial sense of purpose as articulated in St. John's. This delicate balance must constantly be struck in all areas of development, if the uniqueness of Newfoundland is to flower as it should with each passing year. And ultimately, there is the challenge of completing the dream of Confederation – a generous and spiritually rewarding Confederation – in the fullness of time.

2

In 1979, I was asked by the Board of Governors of St. Francis Xavier University to accept the chairmanship of a Campaign for Excellence which was designed to raise $7 million. I accepted because the cause was worthy and the needs were great.

This university was founded to fill a special kind of need. It was built over 130 years ago by the sacrifice of farmers, fishermen, and coal miners in eastern Nova Scotia because they wanted a place to provide their children with a good education and an equal opportunity in life. It was built, too, on the unremitting commitment of the local clergy who, with their secular colleagues, made of St. F.X. a monument to free thought, a garden of tolerance, an instrument of academic accomplishment, and a school with a social conscience.

The splendid legacy of St. F.X. is, in many ways, a simple story of uncommon service to others – the growth of co-operatives designed to provide easier access to a common source of community financing; the Extension Department, which gave true meaning to the concept of self-help and which provided trade unionism with noble goals and genuine assistance; the Coady International Institute, designed to improve standards of living of people in developing countries; and the education of successive generations of students who were formed in this atmosphere and rendered more gentle and caring as a result.

I know from personal experience that few people can be educated at St. F.X. and emerge untouched by these values. Dr. Moses M. Coady, a giant figure on this campus and a true leader of men, said it clearly in 1939, the year I was born:

> We have no desire … to create a nation of mere shopkeepers whose thoughts run only to groceries and to dividends. We want our men to look into the sun and into the depths of the sea. We want them to explore the hearts of flowers and the hearts of fellow men. We want them to live, to love, to play and pray with all their being. We want them to be men, whole men, eager to explore all the avenues of life and to attain perfection in all their faculties. We want for them the capacity to enjoy all that a generous God and creative men have placed at their disposal. We desire above all that they will discover and develop their own capacities for creation.

When I was young in Baie Comeau, the good gentlemen of the Ivy League were not knocking at anyone's door. St. F.X. took me in and gave me the moorings, the philosophy, and the opportunity.

I undertook the responsibility of raising funds both in gratitude for all the university had done for me and for so many others in similarly precarious financial circumstances. I took it as well in recognition of those whose constant sacrifice kept the flame of concern for one's fellow men alive over so many years. It must never be extinguished.

We have surpassed the $7 million objective. I turn over to you today the amount of $11.1 million raised by a remarkable group of fellow alumni and volunteers across Canada, which I had the pleasure of leading, and who have worked tirelessly for three years to bring about this reality today. It is our way of thanking you, the university community – faculty, students, and staff – for your contribution both to the principle of academic excellence and to the betterment of conditions for the less privileged in our society. I am honoured to be in your company.

Chapter XII
The Conservative Challenge

1

Pierre Elliott Trudeau has been in power longer than all Conservative leaders combined since the end of World War I. Think of it for a moment. Mr. Trudeau will have been more successful – in terms of prime-ministerial longevity – than Messrs. Meighen, Bennett, Manion, Bracken, Drew, Diefenbaker, Stanfield, and Clark put together.

With few if any exceptions, the Conservative Party has been consigned to the Opposition benches for one reason alone – its failure to win seats in the French-speaking areas of the nation. From northern and eastern Ontario through Quebec and into northern New Brunswick, the electorate has rejected the Conservative Party with a consistency that is at once staggering and overwhelming.

The reasons? Well, take your pick – Louis Riel, conscription, poor organization, Quebec lieutenants, no provincial party, poor policy, unilingual leaders, two-nation theories – take your pick, but make it soon because we are running out of excuses. We may have none to offer if we hesitate too long.

A good excuse is like the problem of the chicken or the egg. It goes something like this: "If only we could squeeze into power, then in the following election Quebecers would vote for us because they love a bandwagon and we could then build a Quebec wing."

In the last election, with the Progressive Conservatives in power, we declined to our lowest ebb in thirty-five years, winning but one seat and 12.6 per cent of the popular vote. In fact, in the seventy-five Quebec ridings, fifty-four candidates lost their deposits completely. Our candidates ran third in forty-one seats, behind the NDP in thirty-nine seats, and even behind the Rhinoceros Party in two.

I have worked steadily on behalf of the Conservative Party since I became a member more than twenty-five years ago. I recall with pleasure the talented, thoughtful, and hard-working men and women I have come to know well in the Party, both in Quebec and across the country. And I regret that the nation has been deprived of their services in government, generation after generation, because our weakness in French Canada has turned the country into a one-party state.

I particularly grieve for that small contingent of courageous Quebecers who have stood firmly for the Party over the years, silently suffering the friendly jeers of their neighbours and the unalloyed scorn of their political adversaries. All of them, I think, deserve the Order of Canada on the basis of their service both to country and to Party. They have received, instead, the unenthusiastic tolerance reserved by the Party hierarchy for those hapless ne'er-do-wells whose only role of substance is to visibly perpetuate the myth that the Conservative Party is truly national in scope, authority, and representation. A similar indictment of the Liberals in this regard, because of their failure in the West, is no less accurate but much less compelling on account of the often fragile linguistic make-up of the nation.

In the Liberal Party, Quebecers have always played key and substantive roles of leadership. Voters are not stupid; they know this. Such is not the case with the Conservatives; and the voters know this, too. So where are the Trudeaus, Lalondes, Chrétiens, Marchands, Pelletiers, and Drurys of the Conservative Party in Quebec? They are here, every bit as talented, dynamic, and able. They are called Dupras, Danis, Masse, Léger, Blanchard, Holden, and Finestone – to name but a few; and they are largely unknown and unheralded because they did not make it to the House of Commons; because they carry on their political backs the heavy mortgage imposed on Conservative candidates by generations of failure. The two individuals who won seats for the Tories here on a consistent basis, Messrs. LaSalle and Grafftey, should patent their remarkable elixir and peddle the stuff indiscriminately to Conservatives in Quebec and Liberals in Alberta. They would make a fortune.

I thought it was impossible for anyone to work harder than former leader Robert Stanfield to win the favour of Quebec. The leadership and understanding he showed on the great issues that confronted our country at the time were outstanding. And I remember as well the frustrations and heartache—indeed the guilt—we in the Quebec Party felt when, in 1972, a few more seats would have meant the difference. So, by the narrowest of margins, we got another Liberal government and another historic reversal of position on a fundamental issue—this time, wage-and-price controls.

I do not know what Mr. Stanfield would have done as Prime Minister. I feel certain, however, that his administration would have been both principled and progressive, and that his accomplishments would have been genuinely good for Canada. The same is true of Joe Clark. Who knows what benefits might have been visited upon the country had he been given the opportunity to govern longer? Instead, the life of his young government was smothered in one of the most cynical acts of political infanticide in Canada's history. In the following election, the promise of change and the renewal of hope—so vital in a democracy—were quickly extinguished and the process of restoration swiftly completed.

And so, as a young and talented new generation of Quebecers begins its inexorable drift to the Liberal Party and the age-old process continues, thoughtful Conservatives in Quebec sometimes pause and wonder about how it might have been.

2

Though the prospect is daunting, the challenge is clear. The duty of the Conservative Party is to deal on a priority basis with this, its major problem. Everything else pales into relative insignificance because Canadians will not entrust their governance to people they perceive as not having come to grips with a problem that is basic to their ongoing existence. When you strip away the partisan rhetoric, the occasional intolerance, the bitching about bilingual corn flakes boxes, and the boos because the national anthem is sung in either English or French or both at a baseball game—when you get right down to it, Canadians want above all else to remain together, united in one of the most successful and fortunate political groupings in recorded history.

When a Canadian votes, he wants a government that is going to represent all provinces and both major linguistic groups because he knows that the absence of some may jeopardize the rights of many. We must all be heard, and ultimately as Canadians we will support that party with which we can comfortably identify because it best articulates our aspirations. So the Conservative Party must begin again the hard and sometimes painful work required to convince the Canadian people that it deserves to govern as an unquestioned national political grouping because it has, in fact, become one; begin again the process that will enable it to earn trust and acceptance from the only place in the country it has been denied.

The words of Santayana are worth remembering: "Those who cannot remember the past are condemned to fulfil it." So what must be done? In my view, the following points should be considered by the Party. They do not constitute a panacea. They are, however, consistent with the old Chinese proverb that "a voyage of a thousand miles begins with a single step."

1. A vigorous provincial Conservative Party must be established in Quebec. You cannot have nine-tenths of a national party and expect to form governments on a regular basis representing ten-tenths of the population.

2. The Party must proceed immediately to nominate twenty candidates a year in anticipation of the next election. Good men and women chosen now, representative of their milieu, active in Caisses Populaires, Centraide, and school-board work, will give the Party the human and sympathetic local dimension it lacks, and will give the candidates the time to nurture fragile Conservative roots in barren areas across this province.

3. These candidates must be supported morally and financially by the national Party. A grant formula whereby five dollars nationally is contributed to match every dollar raised within the constituency, repeated visits by the national leader, senior caucus members, and provincial Premiers would do much to provide the candidate with encouragement and credibility. One hundred dollars spent today on behalf of such a candidate is infinitely more productive than $5,000 thrown willy-nilly into a riding on behalf of a parachuted candidate three weeks before a general election.

4. Some of these new candidates should be invited to attend all national caucus and organizational meetings on a regular basis as

ex-officio members. This would provide the national Party with the Quebec input on sensitive issues it so sorely lacks and give new candidates the benefit of frequent association with and exposure to our experienced parliamentary troops.

5. Small policy conventions should be held on a regional and sectoral basis throughout the province. Pulp and paper, textiles, and mining are less glamorous subjects of debate than communications and foreign affairs. But they are industries on which the well-being of entire regions depends, and the Conservatives must identify with people in these regions and with their problems.

6. A membership drive must be launched. By and large the Party does not even know its dwindling membership. Communication with its supporters is tenuous at best. The objective should be modest but significant growth. Each riding should recruit 100 new members a year until the next general election. This would provide the Party with 30,000 new card-carrying members when the next writ is issued, which is about 25,000 more than we have at present.

7. Top Quebecers, francophone Ontarians, and Acadians should be sought out for major leadership roles in the Leader's Office, National Headquarters, National Association, and all decision-making bodies in the Party. The traditional roles of "assistant to," "deputy of," and "second vice-president" no longer suffice. The era of *Le Roi Nègre*, as poignantly described by André Laurendeau, is over.

To the extent humanly possible, I make these comments in the genuine belief that they are devoid of partisanship. It is unhealthy for the present situation to persist; unhealthy for you and me and for the political process, to say nothing of the country itself. We all benefit from reasonable challenge and change. We all lose when our governors resist new ideas and attitudes simply because they have quietly come to believe that only theirs have merit and only they can produce the numbers that add up to a government. It is difficult not to become disdainful of the tenant when one has owned the plantation for decades.

The talent and wisdom in the Conservative caucus and Party are not to be underestimated. When confronted with a grave problem they are capable of appropriate remedial action. It is important to all of us that they address this problem in an urgent and sustained manner. We know there are no simple solutions. We know as well that there are few problems incapable of resolution, given the proper application of time, innovative energy, and good faith.

If the Conservatives succeed in this initiative, we will assume office on a regular basis with ample opportunity to implement those policies we deem beneficial to Canada. If we fail, we can kiss the occasion good-bye.

For my part, I believe that success in this area will come because the Party—its people, policies, and perceptions of the magnificence of Canada—will itself have come to exemplify qualities we all most admire and dreams we most cherish for our families, our country, and ourselves.

Chapter XIII
Change and Challenge

This book, presenting some of my speeches over recent years, is a record of my thoughts both on issues of the day and on the broader concerns of the times in which we are living. Woven throughout this book is a vision, my vision of our country, of our greatness, its troubles, its past, and particularly of the future that awaits us if we can only learn from our past the lessons offered to us there.

I would like, in concluding this book, to summarize here the lessons I have learned and the future that I believe can be ours.

The Progressive Conservative government I envision is one that has a real understanding of all Canada – its accomplishments and its potential place in today's changing world. We must always keep in mind the tremendous challenges that are reshaping economic activity throughout the world. We in Canada have to appreciate the international forces that influence and press upon us. As a trading nation in a highly competitive world environment, economic and social events are impacting on us in ways that will fundamentally alter long-established institutions and habits we have come to take for granted. These factors can be managed, but they must first be understood.

There has always been economic rivalry between countries or regions, but there are now new factors:

- Large-scale mass production industries are shifting to lower wage countries.
- The proportion of world income generated from the sale of natural resources is declining.
- Financial capital is more internationally mobile. Investment

funds flow wherever there are profitable opportunities.

- Industrialized countries are increasingly reliant on developing, acquiring, and applying high technology for their competitive advantage – high technology meaning a high rate of change combined with a high knowledge content.
- The future strength of industrialized and developing countries will depend on the quality and skills of human resources because people are the key to harnessing technology and fostering creativity and innovation.

Under these growing pressures, and particularly in times of recession, shares of world trade become a principal cornerstone of economic policy by developed nations and by Third World nations alike. As the competition intensifies the spirit of GATT tends to be forgotten, trade barriers go up, and the vicious circle of protectionism chokes off our collective opportunities for recovery.

For Canadians, with over 30 per cent of our GNP devoted to trade, increasing global protectionism is totally contrary to our economic well-being. As the rivalry mounts among the major trading blocs of the United States, Japan, and the European Economic Community, we must view with alarm the damaging consequences to ourselves and others of orchestrated restrictions to the flow of trade. Although we have to work in the world as it is and cannot afford the Boy Scout role, we nevertheless must energetically stand and press for the lowering of barriers to trade because trade is our lifeblood. In that direction lies our future prosperity. Government in Canada must see its role as creating with the private sector a greater and freer access to world markets and higher levels of trade.

On this critical issue of trade, the Liberal regime has served us badly over the last two decades. Even in the boom years when overall world trade was growing, Canada's share of trade dropped by 33 per cent, which was the worst performance of all the industrial countries. In every area, from food and primary products to high value-added goods, we have lost market share. Because each percentage point of trade means $6.5 billion, the effect of these Liberal policy failures on Canadian employment can be easily seen and painfully felt.

Access to world trade is therefore a top priority for us. We must revitalize our efforts and sharply reverse the performance of recent years. Canada is part of a tougher, changing world, and it is time we began to understand and deal with that fact.

It is absolutely clear that the private sector is and must continue to be the driving force in the economy. It is not a matter of whether government or the private sector should take the lead in rejuvenating the economy. In this context of intensifying competition, the role and purpose of government policy will relate primarily to how we can nurture and stimulate the Canadian private sector. A Progressive Conservative government will create an overall economic environment which provides exactly this kind of support. Such an effort will relate not only to high-technology enterprises, but to raising productive capacity in the entire range of companies in every sector and at every level.

What is called for is a new capacity in government to bridge the middle ground between all sectors of the economy. For twenty years, Canada has seen a growth and style of government which has led to more and more intervention. Rather than bringing the country together and building prosperity, this record of intervention has dampened the spark of private initiative and divided the country. The task before us will be a big one. We must create new conditions that will encourage private sector initiatives, which in turn will ensure Canada's future.

There are internal, domestic Canadian realities a Conservative government will need to be ready to face. Trade barriers exist here at home, between provinces and regions. The emphasis on a central Canada manufacturing policy has engendered an unnecessary divisiveness. Unco-ordinated policies for large and for small business have not helped to create a sense of unified purpose; the low level of research and development has hampered industrial progress. Confrontation between Ottawa and business, and Ottawa and organized labour, has destroyed the collaboration on which real productivity advances are based.

We have seen Ottawa almost consciously pitting itself against industry as a rival in the economy. Our major commitment will be to get the respective roles of the two sectors clearly in focus. The private sector in Canada, embracing both employee and employer, industry and labour, is the engine of the Canadian economy and must accept responsibility for that role. Government's role is to

98

support that entrepreneurial effort; not to replace it, not to hamper it, but to help it in every way possible to become effective in the national and international marketplace. No matter what the industrial circumstances or ad hoc justifications, there is something wrong about the existence of some 600 Crown corporations. The private sector must have room to breathe and room and energy to grow. Government's role is to provide that environment.

What we will provide in the relationship between government and the private sector is a new kind of leadership – leadership at the national level, which in turn will stimulate entrepreneurship among people and organizations, in all sectors of the economy. I accept the legitimate differences of all groups and individuals in society – that is part of my conservative convictions. But I wish to recognize the opportunities for reconciling and mending the growing divisiveness in Canada that Liberal policies have created. It is this divisiveness between legitimate interests which is really holding us back – federal-provincial, east-west, business-labour, large and small business, and English- and French-speaking communities.

For a country such as Canada, concert and consensus are not easily accomplished. But whatever method we use, most emphatically we cannot solve the problem by imposing a view from Ottawa. The fundamental policy mistake of the Liberal regime has been to see diversity as a problem rather than an important asset. Because of that we have seen and suffered from a confrontation designed to impose conformity, rather than a genuine dialogue patiently conducted and constructively pursued to produce broad consensus.

In this tougher, faster-paced, more competitive world, the management of change can be achieved only by encouraging openness and dialogue rather than by suppressing them; by tapping the advantages and energies of diversity rather than by seeking to stamp them out, and by promoting exchange rather than provoking argument.

To take but one example, the interests of large and small business are highly interdependent. In the competitive and rapidly changing world of today, small and medium enterprise generates creativity, produces momentum, provides jobs, and builds the national economy. We cannot succeed as a nation if the private sector is frustrated and hobbled by a government that does not understand the entrepreneurial role of this sector.

This situation will be even more true in the next decade than it was in the past. Large corporations increasingly rely on small, efficient, competitive suppliers. As world competition increases, new ideas will need to be generated and commercialized more rapidly. As technological leadership becomes more critical, creative enterprises will fuel economic growth.

The central policy challenge is to secure effective linkages among governments, financial institutions, well-established business, and the community of entrepreneurs. What is needed is not one policy thrust for large corporations and another for small, but rather a flexible framework that recognizes the entrepreneurial character of both large and small companies. Clearly, in Canada that policy thrust has been sorely missed for the last twenty years.

The mutually reinforcing relationship between large and small business can have a positive impact on small as well as large communities across Canada. At present many smaller Canadian communities depend solely on resource industries – farming, fishing, mining, forestry. Canada can continue to build on this resource wealth and diversity, but the opportunities for these communities in attracting or starting new industries – firms such as Mitel, Atco, and Bombardier – will grow as the Canadian economy restructures in an entrepreneurial direction. It is up to all of us to make this happen.

Whatever we have been led to believe in these recent decades of dispute, every sector of Canadian society – small and big business, labour, the regions, ethnic groups, all of us – wants a stronger Canada.

Nurturing that willingness and commitment must be the major concern of Conservative leadership. In its absence, the changes and challenges of the competitive world will prove to be insurmountable obstacles. Given a constructive diversity, Canadians may achieve the productivity and potential which our resources and energies merit. The task of leadership is to help generate that opportunity.

Fifty years ago it was said, with pride and optimism, that the twentieth century would belong to Canada. Canada, we believed, was about to take its place at the head of the free, prosperous, proud, and benevolent countries of the world. We have fallen short of these expectations.

But we can learn. We can reverse these ominous trends and once again secure for Canada the future it deserves.

We need new ideas, new visions, to replace the notions that have so tragically misguided and deflected us from the future our fore-fathers planned and dreamed.

By learning from the past, and finding a new vision for the future, we can begin to build the free, prosperous, and humane destiny that we all seek, both for ourselves and for the country we serve.

Acknowledgements

The chapters of this book express my thoughts and feelings about Canada and about some of the most pressing problems that face Canadians today. Each chapter has been based on an address, or addresses, delivered during the last number of years to audiences in different parts of the country. For these invitations and opportunities to present and develop my views, I wish to thank the officers and members of the organizations and associations listed below.

Chapter I. Address to the Ottawa-Carleton Federal Progressive Conservative Association Fund-raising Dinner, Holiday Inn, Ottawa, Ont., April 22, 1982.

Chapter II. Address to the Canadian Institute of Mining and Metallurgy, Holiday Inn, St. John's, Nfld., November 8, 1981.

Chapter III. Address to the Broadview-Greenwood Progressive Conservative Association Fund-raising Dinner, Weston Hotel, Toronto, Ont., May 5, 1982.

Chapter IV. Address at the Brunch of the Progressive Conservative Association of the Constituency of Louis Hébert, Auberge des Gouverneurs, Ste-Foy, Quebec, October 10, 1982.

Chapter V. Address to the North Vancouver-Burnaby Progressive Conservative Association Fund-raising Dinner, Hotel Vancouver, Vancouver, B.C., May 17, 1982.

Chapter VI. Address at the Testimonial Dinner to Celebrate the Tenth Anniversary of Election to the House of Commons of Otto Jelinek, MP, Oakville, Ont., November 10, 1982. Address to the Fund-raising Dinner, St-Denis Progressive Conservative Association, Hyatt Regency Hotel, Montreal, Quebec, March 14, 1982.